Straight Women, Gay Men

Straight Women, Gay Men

Absolutely Fabulous Friendships

Robert H. Hopcke and Laura Rafaty

WILDCAT CANYON PRESS
A Division of Circulus Publishing Group, Inc.
Berkeley, California

Straight Women, Gay Men:
Absolutely Fabulous Friendships

Copyright 1999 by Robert H. Hopcke and Laura Rafaty

Cover photo by Stone/Chris Craymer

Publisher: Tamara Traeder
Editorial Director: Roy M. Carlisle
Marketing Director: Carol Brown
Managing Editor: Leyza Yardley
Production Coordinator: Larissa Berry
Copyeditor: Jean M. Blomquist
Cover Design: Mary Beth Salmon
Interior Design: Candace Bieneman
Typesetting: Margaret Copeland/Terragraphics

Typographic Specifications: Body text set in 11.5 pt Bodoni Book; Heads set in Bodoni Bold Condensed and Bodoni Demi-Bold

Printed in the United States of America

Library of Congress Cataloging in Publication Data
Hopcke, Robert H. 1958–

    Straight women, gay men : absolutely faboulous friendships / by Robert H. Hopcke and Laura Rafaty.

      p.   cm.

    Includes bibliographical references.

    ISBN 1-885171-61-7 (pbk. : alk. paper)

    1. Gay men—Relations with heterosexual women—United States.

    1. Rafaty, Laura. 1958–   . II. Title.

    HQ76.2.U5H67 1999

    306.7—dc21   99-36254

                                        CIP

Distributed to the trade by Publishers Group West
10 9 8 7 6 5 4 3 2 1   01 02 03 04 05

Dedication

To Bryan Batt and Tom Cianfichi, for proving that true love lasts and that it *is* possible to keep one's hairstyle in place through sheer force of personality. And to Tamara Traeder, whose friendship and support made this book possible.

— Laura

To my mother, Gloria Hopcke. May she rest in peace.

— Rob

Contents

Acknowledgments ix ☞

Preface xi ☞

A Most Remarkable Friendship 1 ☞ A Word About Stereotypes and Generalizations 11 ☞ We Don't Have a Split Personality (And Neither do We) 13 ☞ Let's Talk about Us for a Minute 14 ☞

1. Choosing Each Other 19 ☞ Let's Be Friends 20 ☞ The Benefits of Work 22 ☞ Getting Crazy 27 ☞ Retail Therapy and Sports 34 ☞ The Essentials of a Civilized Life 37 ☞ Superficiality Runs Deep 45 ☞

2. Talking To Each Other 52 ☞ Speaking Freely 58 ☞ Ten Great Lies 68 ☞

3. Coming Out as the Moment of Truth 74 ☞ Begin at the Beginning 75 ☞ Let Me Tell You Something 81 ☞ No, Let *Me* Tell *You* Something 88 ☞ Bridges to the Past 93 ☞ The Big Secret 99 ☞

4.   Playing the Field ... Together 102 ☞ Picking Up Signals 106 ☞ For What It's Worth... 110 ☞ Dishing the Dirt and Other Pastimes 116 ☞ Meet Mr. Right 120 ☞

5.   Romancing Each Other 124 ☞ Getting Sentimental! 127 ☞ Emotional Bravery 129 ☞

6.   Keeping Secrets From One Another 135 ☞ The Forbidden Topic 136 ☞ Unveiling the Mystery 145 ☞

7.   Flirting With Each Other 150 ☞ The Attraction Factor 151 ☞ The Generosity Quotient 159 ☞ Honey, Drape! 163 ☞ A Very Rich Stew 167 ☞

8.   Testing the Limits of Love 172 ☞ Seeing the Dark Side 180 ☞ Projection's Place 189 ☞

9.   Dealing with People's Reactions 196 ☞ Family Dynamics 198 ☞ The Jealous Boyfriend 203 ☞ Here Comes Homophobia 207 ☞

10. Defending Each Other: Fag Hags and other Stereotypes 215 ☞ The Charming Epithet 217 ☞ The Power of Insult 222 ☞ Telling It Like It Is 230 ☞

11. Being There for Each Other 234 ☞ Facing AIDS Together 236 ☞ Dealing With Other Life Crises Together 242 ☞

12. Understanding Each Other 245 ☞ The Gift of Acceptance 250 ☞ A Larger Vision 252 ☞

Notes 255 ☞

About the Authors 256 ☞

About the Press 257 ☞

Authors' Note

In certain instances, names and circumstances in this book have been changed to protect the privacy of individuals.

Acknowledgments

It is a great pleasure to work with the folks at Wildcat Canyon, people who love books and know how to support their authors. We extend to them all our thanks and appreciation for many hours of hard work, discussion and laughter.

— Rob & Laura

I would like to thank the people I interviewed for this book who shared a great deal of their lives with me but who for reasons of privacy will not be mentioned by name. You know who you are, and I appreciate your candor, time and enthusiasm for this book. Likewise, I would like to express my deep gratitude for my family and friends: each book has its own set of demands and you all keep me sane, grounded and human.

— Rob

I wish to thank all of the friends, acquaintances and innocent bystanders who agreed to be interviewed for this book. I also thank Michele Faulkner for her guidance, Patrick Stucky for his wisdom, my professional colleagues in New York and California for their support, and most particularly the fabulous Jake Beasley for his invaluable contributions to the book, editorial and otherwise. The most difficult thing about this project is not being able to thank by name so many of my other dear friends who shared their stories with me, but who for reasons of privacy cannot be mentioned. Your loyalty, honesty and bravery continue to amaze.

— Laura

Preface

A New Recognition

When the first edition of this book was written, the relationship between straight women and gay men was largely invisible to the mainstream media. Since that time, several major film studios have released movies based on this friendship, including *The Object of My Affection* and *The Next Best Thing*, and mainstream television shows from *Dawson's Creek* to *All My Children* have given the relationship an unprecedented focus. New portrayals of these friendships differ from past versions in two significant ways. First, the friendship is often integral to a principal story line, not an aside. Second, the friendship is shown as healthy and empowering rather than dysfunctional (although filmmakers still manage to hit every stereotype of the friendship and to tend toward its dark side – as anyone who saw Madonna and Rupert's characters conceive a child in a night of drunken abandon can testify). Even more telling, the friendships are often portrayed without any fuss; no one labels them as extraordinary or even refers to the fact of the gay man-straight woman partnership. As in life, the friendship is shown to arise naturally in the course of the storyline that comprises the lives of the characters.

Most encouraging, however, is the triumph of a then-struggling little television series we referenced in the first edition of this book: *Will & Grace*. W&G has since become a breakout hit, won (among numerous prizes) the Emmy for best comedy in 2000 and for best supporting actor and actress, and was rewarded by the network with a coveted spot on its Must-See-TV Thursday night lineup. The show features dead-on portrayals of the many facets of the friendship between straight women and gay men, from the healthy to the histrionic to the hilarious. For the first time, such friends can tune in and see themselves and their own friendships in every episode, whether reflected in the more traditionally loving friendship of the title characters, or in the over-the-top excesses of Karen and Jack, the two "supporting" characters (a term that hardly fits them in any respect). Make no mistake: this is a network show which in its early days made what some viewers regarded as compromises. Will's character was a fairly "straight" gay man who was rarely portrayed as overtly sexual. Grace's romantic obsession with Will was milked to create forced sexual tension between them on an early season's cliffhanger. Ironically, however, it was the high camp portrayals of the supporting characters, with their overt sexuality, excesses of ego and alcohol, and mutually lust-laden interaction that propelled the series' reputation and ratings. Accordingly, it appears that the more successful the show, the bolder the writers have become, and the show and its four talented stars continue to push the envelope in portraying the friendship with startling accuracy to hilarious effect.

Whether in the media or in our lives, these friendships are all around us. After the first edition was published, we met enthusiastic readers everywhere. "You're writing about us!" they would say. "This is just like our friendship." And surprisingly, straight men wanted to know: "What can I learn about women from their gay friends?" Since this friendship has suddenly taken center stage, let's take a closer look.

A Most Remarkable Friendship

 "Can men and women ever really be friends?" If we're talking about a gay man and a straight woman, the answer is a resounding "yes!" Most women today have at least one close friend or confidante who is

One quality stands out as the hallmark of this relationship: a shared sense of fun, the outrageous, and the unpredictable.

a gay man, and gay men frequently have a number of close friends who are straight women. The friendship between these two may be one of the closest, but most complex, in their lives. Gay men often describe their straight female friend as the one person most ready to accept their sexual orientation, while straight women often say that their gay male friend is more supportive and nurturing, and less judgmental, than his straight counterparts. And one quality stands out as the hallmark of this relationship: a shared sense of fun, the outrageous, and the unpredictable.

Whether they are commiserating about love lives, trying to figure out which "team" a desirable man "plays for," or getting the insider's perspective on what men or women really think, straight women and gay men can always turn to one another for the straight scoop on the opposite sex. And they can always count on each other to say "you look fabulous," "thinner," or "younger" — whichever is needed. Yet these friendships should never be confused with relationships between girlfriends or male buddies. While they are clearly platonic, these friendships may involve mutual attraction, sexual tension, and even romantic love. Many gay men enjoy strong friendships with straight women who are former girlfriends. Gay men and straight women often share intimate secrets only with one another, while keeping important parts of their lives separate. Still one quality seems to distinguish the relationship: the tolerant, accepting, unconditional love that makes this relationship unique, yet universal.

In an era when men and women are supposed to be from "different planets" and unable to communicate with each other, gay men and straight women seem able to communicate almost effortlessly. Perhaps it is because this is not a relationship undertaken out of convenience or forced by societal pressure, but one that is carefully chosen on the basis of common interests, mutual respect and real affection. Or perhaps it is because, freed from the stereotypical male-female roles, gay men and straight women can relate to one another simply as people.

We will be celebrating here the importance of the friendship between gay men and straight women and the effect of this friendship on their lives. We will also be addressing the changing perception of this friendship in society, which used to disparage or marginalize this relationship, but which increasingly recognizes it as one of the most enduring and enjoyable friendships two people can share. But most of all, we wish to honor that special friendship which enables us to live our lives with grace, laughter and, above all, style!

Our own friendship was born in the course of writing this book together, and, through it, we realized that both of us shared certain basic feelings. First, we both believe that any friendship, whether casual or deep, is a rare and valuable enhancement to anyone's life; none of us can thrive without the goodwill, affection, shared pleasure, generosity and support that we get from our friends. Second, we think that the special things that bring straight women and gay men together as friends deserve to be understood and held up for attention within a culture that often misperceives the actual experience of women and gay people. Finally, we both discovered through our conversations and our writing that a whole lot can be learned (or unlearned) about relationships in general from this particular sort of friendship.

We spent a year or so gathering up the real-life experiences of women and gay men regarding their loving relationships with each other. To other people's stories, we added a lifetime of our own friendships, which makes this book more than just a celebration of this relationship. We both wanted this book to be a thorough and thoughtful exploration of what such friendships *mean* to those of us who share them. The topic, in our opinion, requires more than a compendium of "feel good" stories and trite conclusions, an approach that would only further shortchange a relationship already misunderstood. The questions posed by this sort of friendship are serious ones: why do we love whom we love? How does the society we live in affect our friendships? What does it mean to be a woman or a man? Is understanding possible between people who are very different? The answers to these questions may well hold a lesson for all who want to be friends with another person, regardless of sexual orientation.

When we turned from our interviews to written resources, we did not find much. Very little of a serious nature is written on friendship in general, and while we did find some thoughtful writing on the relationship between lesbians and gay men (which is one of the reasons we do not cover that topic here), we noticed a definite lack of writing on friendships between gay men and straight women. This scarcity reveals how little friendship is valued in our modern day. Once upon a time, friendships of all sorts received a great deal of attention from philosophers, thinkers, writers, and poets. Today, however, it seems that the ideal of romantic, passionate, erotic, and sexual love between straight men and women has become practically the *only* model of relationship recognized as socially valuable, appropriate, or desirable. (We could even call this a form of "relationship fetishism.") In fact, in everyday speech, the very word "relationship" — which should be a general term for the nearly infinite forms of human interaction — has become practically synonymous with a love relationship, as in "I'm not in a relationship right now," "I've just begun a relationship with a great guy," or "I don't feel right when I'm not in a relationship." In our opinion, to shrink the meaning of the word "relationship" in this way impoverishes both our language and emotional lives. While many of us may not be in romantic love relationships at any given time in our lives, we all may enjoy a plethora of other relationships. The relationships we share with our friends, our families, our co-workers and our neighbors can be as loving and as sustaining for us — perhaps even more loving and sustaining than — as any hot-and-heavy romance.

For this reason, this book challenges the notion that romance is the end-all-and-be-all of human experience. Romantic love relationships have their place; we all know love is grand, but our friends are often the ones who keep us sane, human, and grounded in our deepest selves.

On the face of it, friendships seem easily explained as a coincidence between proximity and common interests. We become friends with people near us who share what moves us, delights us, inspires us, or pains us, which means that a wide variety of relationships may be termed "friendships." On the one hand, there are the friendships we have with those whom life has thrown by chance across our literal physical paths — the people who live across the street, our roommates, the folks that we work with, all the people who may or may not share much in common with us as far as interests go but with whom, over time, we develop a bond. Based more on geography than psychology, these friendships are like the grass in the garden of our emotional lives — plentiful, green and very grounding but also sometimes patchy and not very deeply rooted.

On the other hand, friendships born of common interests rather than mere physical proximity flower with a deeper, more vibrant, and more enduring color. These are the friends we have grown up with, gone to school with, double-dated with — people who have chosen to remain close to us. They've stuck with us during financial hardships, divorce, death and disappointments. They've been there to share equally in our good fortune, marriages, births and triumphs. With these friends, we share a common outlook, a set of values, and a history that transcend distance or separation. We may not talk to each other for months or even years, yet when we pick up the phone and hear that familiar voice or get together for dinner, it feels like just yesterday when we talked to them last. We turn to these friends first with bad news or happy tidings. We share our hopes and joys, as well as our frustrations and our disappointments, with them. Because these friendships are deeper, such friends also tend to be fewer in our lives. Returning to the image of the garden, such friends are like the flowers and trees — less common but more prominent and more beautiful.

In addition to proximity and common interests, there is a very important third factor in friendships, a quality that especially pertains to friendships between gay men and straight women. People become friends because of a "soul connection" between them. One great myth of our culture is that a "soul mate" can only be someone with whom one shares romantic or erotic passion. But the stories of friendship that follow reveal the fallacy of this notion. Indeed, in the wonderful friendships between straight women and gay men, we found that many of the barriers present in other relationships

— the sexual tension, the social pressures, the stupid, petty competitiveness between women or men — are all conspicuously absent. This seems to enable straight women and gay men to bond more quickly and deeply, and results in many of us feeling like we have indeed found a soul mate in our friend, someone who really, truly and deeply understands us.

The women we interviewed about their gay male friends made it abundantly clear again and again that the love they felt for these men — some of whom held places of importance in their emotional lives far beyond any boyfriend or husband — came from a place beyond their heart. They had a passionate feeling toward their gay friends — at times fierce and protective, at other times, simply strong and unshakable — but this passion was clearly not sexual. Similarly, the gay men we spoke to talked of their closest female friends with a level of feeling and emotional commitment that was quite distinct from, and often more vivid than, the way in which they spoke of their own lovers, boyfriends, and even their families. These women hold a very special place in the lives of these men, as do the gay male friends of these women. The unique depth of this friendship, built as it is on a foundation of absolute acceptance, mutual support and unconditional love, is clearly a matter of both heart and soul.

Nowadays, of course, the word "soul" has become fashionable. It is a buzzword in the books that litter the self-help shelves of bookstores, as well as a term that has become more associated with an individual's self-discovery than with one's connection to others. Yet the notion of "soul" has a long religious and cultural tradition that should not be abandoned. We hope that the unique complexity of the friendships we explore here will show us all what "soul" really is and how love, acceptance, and deep commitment can result in a experience of wholeness for two people who still remain, in every sense of the word, friends.

This is why, with intentional ambiguity, we entitled an earlier edition of this book: *A Couple of Friends*. Two friends can indeed be joined to create a "couple," though of a different sort than the term usually implies. They are a couple — a man and a woman — and yet, as is so often the case when gay people are involved, all is definitely not what it seems. What appears to be heterosexual on the surface most definitely is *not* — and yet the pairing of masculine and feminine, man and woman, in these friendships is unmistakably and unquestionably a part of what brings these friends together, often for life. The relationship is platonic in the way that term is usually meant, yet it may have aspects of physical attraction, sexual tension, and romantic affection. They are indeed friends, but they are also, in many ways, more than "just friends" with profound ties to each other on many levels, ties of which even they themselves may not be fully aware. In what follows, we have chosen to look at the various individual elements that make up these friendships and pay attention to each on its own, and so our book has been structured accordingly. By the end, we hope you will have a broader and deeper understanding of your own friendships. We also hope that we will have helped open you up more fully to the marvelous, baffling, amazing complexity of the real nature of love in all its manifestations.

A Word About Stereotypes and Generalizations

In writing this book, we have struggled to avoid stereotypical descriptions of and generalizations about men and women, gay and straight. However, by its very nature, this book draws broad conclusions about a type of relationship that, until now, has been largely unexplored. We, therefore, think it important to state clearly and unequivocally right up front: we know that all men are not one way and all women are not another, and we know that every gay person is a unique individual just as every heterosexual person is. Unfortunately, if we had tried to add "many" "most" or "sometimes" in front of every generalization contained in this book, we would not only have misquoted our interviewees, but our book would have ended up sounding like the work of two exceptionally timid, mealy-mouthed academics. Plus, it would have probably weighed one hundred pounds! So please, indulge us for a time in some gross generalizing and stereotyping in order to facilitate our ability to sketch out, in broad strokes, a depiction of this friendship.

And a special note to straight men: please don't hate us! When you ask women to single out what they find exceptional about gay men, they often do so by drawing a distinction between the behavior of gay men and straight men. Gay men in turn describe certain parts of their lives they find easier to share with straight women than with straight men. And because this book, in comparing straight men and gay men, focuses on the gay men in the equation, they fare better in the comparisons than do their straight counterparts. Of course, it is highly unlikely that hoards of heterosexual men will be stampeding out to buy a book with the word "couple" in the title, much less one with the word "gay " in the subtitle. But for those of you who read this book to learn a bit more about the gay men and straight women in your own lives, we hope you will understand that heterosexual men are not the focus here and so may at times get a bit shortchanged. Our guilt about this, though, is not enormous — after all, straight men have been writing about how superior they are to gay men and straight women for centuries! Oops, there we go again...

We Don't Have a Split Personality (And Neither do We)

We hope you'll understand that throughout our discussion, we sometimes talk as authors, sometimes as individuals, and other times as the subjects of a story we are telling. We've tried to keep it simple by identifying which role we are playing at any given time. But if we shift from the first person to the third, from the individual to the collective, then back again, we trust you'll stay with us. After all, you must be really smart, or you wouldn't be reading this book in the first place. And before you start berating someone whom you think was quoted in this book, or whom you fear may have spilled your most intimate secrets to a couple of authors who would happily plunder their friends' lives for their literary endeavors, bear in mind that most of the names have been changed to protect the privacy of the innocent and to hinder prosecution of the guilty. Speaking of which...

Let's Talk about Us for a Minute

When we started to write this book, we didn't even know one another. Our publisher had the idea for the book, had wanted to do a book with each of us, and so fixed the two of us up on a "blind date" over dinner to explore the possibility of our becoming co-authors. That meeting and our subsequent friendship is a great example of what can happen when you get a gay man and a straight woman together.

On paper, the two of us couldn't be more different. Rob is a licensed marriage and family therapist, living and practicing in Berkeley, California. A best-selling author, he has written a number of books on Jungian psychology, that have ranged from scholarly to popular, and so when he is not seeing clients, he travels extensively to give lectures and workshops on topics as varied as synchronicity, homophobia and opera. Laura is an attorney, corporate executive and writer as well as a Tony-nominated theatrical producer, who has produced theatre on Broadway and elsewhere. She divides her time between the Napa Valley in California and the theatre district in New York, where she hangs out with a bunch of actors and other disreputable types. Rob is a health-conscious gourmet and an athlete – seriously into cycling and working out (at 6 am!). Laura is not – she's less seriously into martinis, seeing all the *good* plays in New York and staying out late. Her athleticism does have a channel: she divides her loyalties between the San Francisco 49ers and the New York Yankees. Rob is a gay man in a twenty-year-long relationship; Laura is a straight woman who is happily single.

Though our initial meeting was arranged, it quickly became clear that we found one another interesting, but since our publishers were there, we couldn't really let loose and kick the tires on one another. We did notice, however, that we seemed to share the same vocabulary and that we got each other's jokes. When Laura made a reference to an Ethel Merman song, Rob was able to sing the refrain — in ear-splitting homage to his idol. When Rob made jokes only a gay man should understand, Laura laughed in all the right places. It was obvious from the start that Rob had a genuine appreciation of and affection for his straight female friends, and Laura felt the same way about her gay male friends. We quickly discovered shared interests in theatre, showtunes and Bette Davis-Joan Crawford movies. We even discovered that we were born one day apart! A partnership was born.

Rob is a serious writer who uses lots of big words like "abstruse" and "propinquity" to prove how smart he is, and thus he was quickly promoted to the position of "chief intellectual" for the partnership. Laura is less ponderous (outside the courtroom or boardroom, anyway), considers the dictionary too heavy to lift, and so was put in charge of making the book fun, entertaining, and delivered in an easy-to-swallow-good-tasting-liquid form. Yet suddenly Laura found herself writing about social pressures, cultural stereotypes and psychological phenomena. Rob, who accuses Laura of "bimbifying" him, suddenly found himself writing about hair mousse, sex toys and drag queens. We brought out the best in one another other, both our silly and serious sides (and the perverse underbellies). To ensure that the book reflected the uninhibited, accepting nature of the friendships between gay men and straight women, we agreed we could talk about *anything*, and we did — from seduction to strip clubs to sperm donors. Rob was willing to tell Laura everything she wanted to know about gay men, Laura was willing to divulge some female trade secrets, and the resulting conversations were honest, uncensored and at times outrageous. We spent many evenings enjoying long dinners and engaging in lively conversation, challenging our assumptions, confounding our expectations, and roaring with laughter. Luckily, we found that while our experiences and our perspectives were often radically different, we could easily see one another's point of view.

And so this book is more than an abstract discussion of friendships between gay men and straight women. It is the direct result of, and the driving force behind, such a friendship. We hope you will consider this book your invitation to join us in this conversation, to pull up your chair, and to take your seat at our dinner table. We trust that what you hear will remind you of your own friendships and will help you to better understand and to truly appreciate the unique nature of the bond between gay men and straight women. And we hope that this book will lead you, as it led us, to something unexpected and delightful: the discovery and appreciation of a true friend.

1. Choosing Each Other

One of the unique aspects of the friendship between gay men and straight women is that they deliberately *choose* each other as friends. There is no social pressure on women to "go out and find themselves a good gay man" nor are gay men disparaged for having too few female friends. Boys are encouraged to "team up" with other boys, and girls are supposed to bond with one

Why then do these two people choose to be together? Probably the most important reason is the simplest: these friends share common interests, tastes, likes and dislikes – and they like to do things together.

another. Particularly in college and later, there is even to a lesser extent some pressure to develop friendships with people from different cultural, religious, or ethnic backgrounds. But there is no such pressure on gay men and straight women to bond, no platonic Valentine's Day, no religious or cultural rituals built around this friendship. Why then do these two people choose to be together?

Probably the most important reason is the simplest: these friends share common interests, tastes, likes and dislikes – and they *like* to do things together. Certainly one of the core ingredients of a friendship — what makes someone a friend — is doing things together. However warmly you may feel toward someone, however intrigued that friend is with you, until you two manage to make some time to share something you both enjoy, the relationship cannot really be called a friendship. The activities we share with our friends lend these relationships their special character.

Let's Be Friends

We found that the friendships between gay men and straight women are, more often than not, born directly out of a shared interest. Ann and Brad met at a new members event at one of the local museums. She remembers, "As we chatted before the speaker began, I realized that the two of us were talking a lot for people who had just met. We seemed to have a lot of mutual interests and found ourselves engaged

Because of their shared interests, their relationship evolved naturally and comfortably into friendship.

in a whole series of enthusiastic exchanges with each other: 'Did you read that book? See that show? What do you think of that artist?' After all this fast talk, I said to myself, 'I like this guy a lot.'

Ann and Brad's friendship grew naturally out of their interest in the arts. As Ann puts it, "I don't remember which of us moved to make it a one-on-one-friendship. Neither of us really, I would say, because we both belonged to this arts group, and at all these events, we ended naturally thrown in together, going to see the same shows, and sitting together or talking about it afterward." Ann and Brad ended up sharing a joint membership in a local lecture series sponsored by a local arts consortium, since neither of their own respective life partners was especially interested in being part of the series.

Likewise, Cynthia and Dave got to know each other through their participation in competitive mahjongg. Cynthia said, "I don't know how long I knew Dave through the mahjongg club, but we played together once, and ever since that time, he has been my primary partner. We go to tournaments together, have our meals together, and share the experience. Our friendship grew from this partnership, since we started getting together for other activities, going to movies together or just spending time with each other."

When talking about the origins of their friendships, neither Ann nor Cynthia could identify one precise moment or special event that marked the beginning of their friendships with Brad and Dave. Because of their shared interests, their relationships evolved naturally and comfortably into friendship.

The Benefits of Work

In addition to the gravitational pull of mutual interests and the appeal of individual personalities, friendships between straight women and gay men can also begin in the workplace, eventually evolving into something more out-side of the professional sphere. Ellen and Frank, for example, were thrown together as new employ-ees at a fledgling account-ing firm on the East Coast where they met on their first day at work. "I had been hired," Ellen recalls, "as their director of human services, and Frank had been hired as

"All sorts of strange things would happen on all levels of the company, but through it all, Frank and I could always go to each other afterward, shake our heads and laugh about it."

one of the managers. At a reception held for new employees, Frank and I got to chatting. One of his responsibilities was to be management liaison with human relations, and one of the big issues the com-pany was dealing with at that time was the matter of discrimination, particularly around sexual orienta-tion." Ellen smiled and added, "As we talked, I found he had — shall we say? — somewhat heated views on the topic."

Ellen and Frank's work responsibilities provided opportunities for frequent contact and conversation. Ellen remembered, "Throughout our first year at the firm, we bonded as we shared experiences in what turned out to be a very odd work environment. All sorts of strange things would happen on all levels of the company, but through it all, Frank and I could always go to each other afterward, shake our heads and laugh about it."

Frank and Ellen's friendship, however, developed into something deeper when they each individually moved to the West Coast. There Frank took Ellen under his wing, so to speak, after she arrived in San Francisco. Ellen recalls, "When Frank left the firm and moved to San Francisco, it turned out I, too, was looking for a change myself. So naturally, when I applied for a position in San Francisco, I contacted Frank before I went out to interview. He was very sweet, and upon my arrival that weekend, insisted on taking me around and showing me the city. This was the point when he formally 'came out' to me and told me he was gay — not that I was surprised, of course. And when I was lucky enough to get the position in San Francisco, Frank was really helpful to me as I moved out there to live. In fact, he actually borrowed a truck and physically helped me move, and during my first year in the city, he was very deliberate in introducing me to his circle of friends."

Ellen laughs as she recalls just how much fun they all had at that time in their lives. "Now remember, this was in the early 1980's, so all his gay friends loved to tease me, saying that I was like Dorothy in the land of Oz, you know, the innocent girl in the wild wonderland of San Francisco. But this whole group of guys and I got together a lot for social stuff, brunches, parties, dinner — you know, those 'simple' home-cooked meals that gay men make — very lavish, very gourmet. I loved those guys, and they were all very sweet and kind to me."

Ellen and Frank's experience of a friendship growing out of a professional connection echoes Rob's experience as well. As a gay man in the largely female field of marriage and family counseling, Rob has had quite a number of women colleagues become close and long-term friends. "People think of psychotherapy as a very male field, but the fact is all the so-called 'helping' professions are very much women's territory, which means most of my interns, students and co-workers are women. In grad school, in fact, out of a class of forty, I was one of three men, and two of us were gay, which gives you a good sense of what it's actually like in the field.

"Naturally, because we therapists tend to be 'people' people, some of my most important and long-lasting friendships have grown out of my professional relationships with women. You work so closely with your colleagues in an agency setting or during supervision, you end up knowing a great deal about each other, and so, you almost always end up continuing that closeness as a friendship. I get together regularly with the half-dozen or so female friends I've made this way — either for lunch to catch up with each other's work and personal lives or by crossing paths at various professional events like seminars or book signings. It's always a delight to see them, and we invariably end up grabbing a cup of coffee and dishing over in the corner."

Similarly, Laura has met a number of her gay friends over the years in her "straight" job as a corporate attorney. "Some of my most cherished friends in corporate boardrooms and courtrooms have been gay. The worlds of law and business often attract people who take themselves too seriously, and it has been such a relief to turn to a gay friend who can see through the pretense and just laugh at pomposity. One of my favorite gay men, a vivacious young man named Seth, worked on the administrative staff of the law firm where I worked, and he would always do things that were totally at odds with the stuffy law firm atmosphere. One year on Halloween, he walked into the office wearing only a gigantic diaper held up by huge blue diaper pins, a big, blue, ruffled bonnet, and a blue satin sash that said, 'It's a Boy!,' and sucking on a gigantic pink pacifier. The expressions on the faces of the partners were priceless, and only he would have had the guts to pull it off. Of all my co-workers, Seth was the most irrepressible and the most fun!"

Getting Crazy

One fabulous aspect of the friendship between gay men and straight women is their ability to bring out one another's zany and outrageous sides. Margaret, a marketing executive, told us this story. "One night, a friend from high school and I were camping out for tickets to a concert. Bob, my friend's coworker, showed up and we just hit it off. We spent the most amazing, silly night in the parking lot of a mall waiting to buy tickets the next

> *"The ability just to be silly with another person is so freeing."*

morning. We stayed up all night, we danced, we did cartwheels across the parking lot, we ran through the fountain. We had one helluva time. The guy who introduced us disappeared from our lives soon after that, but for the next fifteen years Bob and I became inseparable."

Reflecting on their meeting, Margaret said, "What I found attractive about Bob was that he was really fun. I am a really high-energy person, just bouncing off the walls sometimes, and Bob has the energy to keep up with me. There are times when we are reduced to tears laughing over something stupid together. The ability to be silly with another person is so freeing. When you're around a straight man you wish it could be like this – that you could be this free, this casual, and have this much fun with someone who cares about you."

Ellen's outrageous friend Frank, her former co-worker, opened up a whole new world for her when she first moved to San Francisco. She remembers, "Going out for Halloween in San Francisco that first year was a definite eye-opener. Remember, these were the first gay men I had ever really gotten to know well. My friend Frank went as the

Transamerica Pyramid. Another friend was Yogi the Bear, and his lover had this male Mae West thing going on. Then there was this short little guy with a dark mustache who had gotten dolled up — of all things — as Wonder Woman. You can imagine me once I got a load of this crew. I don't know if my eyes could have gotten any bigger." Ellen then added with a laugh, "One thing about it all was quite depressing, though. Most of the guys had better legs than I did!"

Ellen went on to tell another story involving this group of friends: "One Saturday night, we were all together. They decided that they wanted to go to a gay disco in the Haight neighborhood of San Francisco on Sunday morning. They invited me along. 'But I'm going to be in church,' I said, to which they responded simply, "Join us after church, then." So I did. It was certainly a scene! Sunday morning was a little calmer than Saturday night, though some of the people had obviously been there since the night before."

When asked how the experience was for her, Ellen said, "It was a nice warm fall day, and there we were, on the patio out back, listening to the pulsing disco beat of dancing going on inside. It was very much an introduction to another world for me, but I really liked it. It was very relaxed, very fun."

Like Ellen, Laura tends to gravitate toward friends who share her sense of fun and outrageousness, and one of the things Laura most appreciates about her gay friends is that they often share an offbeat sense of humor. "My gay friends tend to be fairly uninhibited. Many of them are performers, and so they tend to be a bit extroverted. Others are directors, writers and artists, and these friends are a bit more shy. But what they all share is an absolutely scathing sense of humor, and the talent to execute some biting satire. Going to the theatre with one friend in particular, especially if the show is bad, is like 'theatre in the round,' as he whispers hilarious commentary into one ear while I listen to the show with the other. After we leave the theatre, he'll perform parodies of what he just saw, and since he is an uncanny mimic, I sometimes double over in laughter. His impression of a wild Jerry Lewis is so hysterical that Jerry Lewis once remarked: 'oh, that kid is *too* good at that.'"

Similarly, one of the things Laura first liked about her friend Alex was his bizarre and wild sense of humor. "For one thing, he kept imaginary pets.

He actually named them, and could always give an anecdote about their behavior; how they had kept him up the night before, how they were always trying to sleep on the bed between him and his boyfriend, all of which was delivered with an absolutely straight face. When Alex and his boyfriend later considered adopting a real pet, I bought them a virtual one — one of those electronic pets you have to feed, water, and walk every few hours. He seemed an attentive virtual pet parent, sharing the duties with his boyfriend, but eventually killed the thing six times. I haven't heard mention of adopting a puppy since."

With a laugh, Laura continues. "Another friend, Chad, pretends that I am his wife to startle and confuse co-workers. We have a secret code I am to use when I call his office: 'Tell him it's his wife calling, and he is late picking up the kids from soccer practice.' This means that he is to meet me at our favorite restaurant for a martini as soon as possible."

"These guys in turn bring out my wild side. One of my gay friends was the stage manager on a show I produced. In order to let an actress who was our assistant stage manager attend an audition, I substituted as the assistant stage manager for the evening performance. My friend was a hilarious tyrant, sending me for coffee and cake, and making rude comments over the headphone as I prepared to execute various sound effects. At the final performance of the run, he egged me from offstage as I flashed my bare chest, covered only by two small stick-on versions of the show's logo, so that the lead actor (my close friend) could see me from on-stage. My gay friends are sometimes a bad influence, and I love them for it."

And since Laura not only produces theatre but is also a Tony voter with a coveted extra ticket to every show on Broadway, she has a built-in excuse to get together with her gay friends who share her passion for good theatre. "I have met some of the most important men in my life through theatre, and many of them are gay. They are my favorite dates at the theatre, because I don't have to explain it to them – they know as much about the subject as I do. Plus, because they also work in theatre, they often know one of the actors or the director, or have played one of the roles in another production, so they can provide special insight, and gossip, that I truly appreciate."

Many gay men and straight women share a strong interest in the arts. For example, Meredith and her friend Mike share a love of music and have created a whole ritual around that. Meredith explains, "One weekend before Christmas Mike and I meet in New York. We go shopping, we see a play, we see movies, and we always see a band. We're both really into music, and we like a lot of the same bands. Over the years we have introduced each other to new bands and music. Meredith smiled and added, "Much of our time together was spent in a car driving, listening to music and singing really loudly."

Meredith and Mike have been friends for many years, and they've shared their friendship as well as their love of music even when times were financially difficult. Meredith told us, "We went to see the Brian Setzer Orchestra years ago when they were first playing at the Supper Club in New York. It was really expensive for us, because we were both broke, but we had a great time – and we can say now that we got to see the band before it got really famous. Now our favorite line which we love to use is, 'Oh, we saw that years ago, *fugeddaboudit*.'"

As illustrated by these stories of how such friendships begin, we all gravitate toward people who take delight in the same things we do or who are curious about similar topics. However, what we found most interesting was to take a look at *what* gay men and straight women friends tended to *do* together.

Retail Therapy and Sports

When we asked the question "What do you do with your friend?" we heard again and again the same sorts of activities being mentioned: going to the movies, theater, or other artistic events; going out to dinner; and going shopping together.

Make no mistake about it: shopping together can, in the right hands, require a near athletic level of consumer prowess.

Make no mistake about it: shopping together can, in the right hands, require a near athletic level of consumer prowess. Margaret and her friend Bob attack flea markets with a well-crafted game plan and flawless execution. Margaret explains, "Bob and I break off so we can scour a whole flea market. I'll say to him, 'Oh, you've got to go over there because they've got this,' and he'll say 'But you've got to go over there because they've got that.' But Bob's also the type who remembers things you are looking for. One day you'll open the mail and there it will be."

Other friends play a "good cop/bad cop" game at flea markets. Dana told us of her shopping ritual with her friend Tom. "I'll be buying something, and he'll wait until the seller and I are clearly haggling over the price. Then Tom will come up and say, 'You can't buy that, where will you put it?'"

There were some exceptions, of course, but while most of the friends we talked to enjoyed shopping and dining, we did not hear many gay men and straight women getting together, for example, to go to football or baseball games, to fix their cars or to build a backyard barbecue. Laura is a big spectator sports fan who has struggled mightily to make fans out of her sports-challenged gay friends for years. "I have thrown several Super Bowl parties and World Series parties over the years, and most of my gay friends could care less about the team, the score or the sport. They come for the alcohol and for my infamous butt-by-butt Super Bowl commentary, but to say that they are uninterested in the game would be an overstatement. Occasionally there will be a cute quarterback; one of my friends once joked that he 'was usually a top, never a bottom, but in the case of Joe Montana wanted to be a center' but that was as close to sports fanaticism as he ever reached. I once had tickets to the musical *Gypsy*, and then was given tickets for the same day to the World Series. There was no question which event I was expected to attend."

Our own friendship tended to confirm this pattern of dining, shopping, and going to the theatre: we went out to dinner to discuss this book — we did not go to a sports bar or to the gym. We went to see a long-running San Francisco drag show send-up of "Mommie Dearest" to celebrate the holidays — we did not go to a rock concert. (This choice, though, may have more to do with our age than with sexual orientation, since we have agreed that we should only attend rock concerts where we are younger than the band.) And Laura insists on going to the gym by herself, mostly to avoid embarrassing public displays of perspiration. Still, for the most part, the two of us, like most gay men and straight women we interviewed, do not share what would traditionally be considered "macho" activities together.

The Essentials of a Civilized Life

Despite the fact that these are male-female couples, the most common activities that these friends share are activities primarily identified with women and in particular, activities in which the stereotypical straight male has little interest. How many wives have to drag their husbands to the bal-

In their friendships with gay men, women get a nearly ideal male partner with whom they can share things that are hard to share with their husbands and boyfriends.

let or theater? How many boyfriends eagerly look forward to a long day shopping in the mall with their girlfriend? Going out to dinner for the heterosexual couple is far less an activity engaged in for its pure aesthetic pleasure as it is a prelude to other activities or as confirmation of a romantic relationship. And many a straight man's heart skips a beat — and not in a good way — when he hears his wife or girlfriend say, "Oh let's just sit and talk. Wouldn't that be romantic?" Even when the man is willing to participate in these activities, he does not necessarily add much to the conversation: Laura knows one straight guy who thinks Art Deco is an old boyfriend of hers. Clearly, in their friendships with gay men, women get a nearly ideal male partner with whom they can share things that are hard to share with their husbands and boyfriends.

We know we are generalizing and there are scads of exceptions, but what we have heard about these friendships and know from our own experience is that the (now somewhat politically incorrect) identification of homosexuality with femininity may not necessarily be a gross error. Obviously, we are not saying that all gay men have an interest in cooking shows, boutiques, and coffee klatches — any more than one can say that all women have an interest in such things. But certainly many gay men do, and for *those* gay men it is a point of contact in their friendships with women.

Yet the question remains: what is it about these activities that make them so interesting to many women? And why do gay men in particular share this interest?

One reason may well be the largely aesthetic character of these activities. Certainly when friends share memberships in museum societies or go to the theater with each other, the connection has to do with the arts. Beauty, the cultivation of beauty and an appreciation of what things look like as opposed to what they do — these have long been a province of the feminine. Of course, depending on one's own attitude toward femininity, to spend time and energy making something look beautiful may be considered trivial and superficial — or, conversely, essential to a civilized life. A figure like Martha Stewart illustrates this point perfectly. By vigorously promoting a way of living that values aesthetic appearance as much as practical utility, she is both enormously popular and relentlessly mocked. Here in the United States, ours is a largely functional culture: things are, first and foremost, supposed to *work*. What they *look* like is secondary. Thus a concern for aesthetics, for beauty, for what is considered inessential, is given over to those who occupy a secondary place in the social hierarchy: women.

To paraphrase an ancient bit of wisdom from Plutarch: luxuries are the only necessities. This delightfully paradoxical insight reveals a powerful secret that women have always known about our culture's obsession with functionality over appearance: namely, to discount the importance of appearance is wrongheaded and silly. Women know the truth that the function of an object — a chair, a meal, a piece of clothing — need never be in opposition to its aesthetic appeal. Indeed, the more attractive, balanced, or appealing something is, the more someone will be drawn to use it. If it pleases both eye and hand, an object has been made *more* practical because it invites people to pick it up and make it a part of their life. A lovely, well-upholstered leather chair, smelling richly, placed in a perfectly lit spot near a big bay window with a view makes you want to curl up in it for the afternoon with a book: its aesthetic appeal enhances its function. A gorgeously set table pulls people in. You want to sit down and smell the flower arrangement. You want to feel the linen napkins, the weight of the silverware. A table set in that manner will have more people gathering around it than the bare ugly wooden table with a cheap plastic cloth and mismatched plastic forks and spoons. Any hat will work to cover your head and keep you warm in the winter, but an especially fetching hat, knit in angora, hugging your ears and turned up smartly at the edges is even more functional because it keeps you warm and makes your round face look angelic, inspiring compliments, attention and admiration.

Women know this secret truth: that the beauty of an object is not a luxurious addition to its basic function but instead is an integral part of its function. And from this secret truth comes a great deal of power. When people make fun of Martha Stewart, they often do so by talking about how power hungry, ambitious and controlling she is — as if this were a stunning revelation about a woman who, after all, commands what has now become a media empire. Only the terminally naive ever believed that between her TV show tapings, her media appearances, and her editing duties at her glossy magazine, Martha personally sat around for hours on end creating new forms of miniature topiary centerpieces for Christmas or that she actually wielded a spade to spread steer manure in her garden. No, this sort of derision, we think, has everything to do with the realization that Stewart knows a powerful secret and that this secret gives her social, cultural and personal leverage. She is aware that how something looks is what often makes it work. Try as we might to resist it with our misguided ascetic Puritan values, the sensual pull of the material world is something that no one can resist. Our senses makes us human. And women like Martha Stewart, if not women in general, do not flinch from using the power of beauty for their own betterment, for the pleasure of others and for the improvement of society in general.

Of course, we recognize that this heightened concern for aesthetic beauty has its shadow side. Laura often bristles against the "tyranny of Marthaism" and its disciples among her gay friends: "Some of my gay friends have much more in common with Martha Stewart and her tribe than I do. This obsession with decor can be annoying. I mean, how many scented candles must one own? As far as these friends are concerned, the invention of electricity was intended solely to power the microwave and the blow dryer. I have had a few gay friends walk into my house or apartment and recoil in horror, not because there was a dead body lying in the middle of my rug, but because the lighting design was considered suboptimal. 'Oh my God — it's so *harsh*!' they scream, as if blue (rather than pink) undertones were carcinogenic. One friend went quietly out to the store for 'supplies' and returned with boxes of 30 watt bulbs which he placed in each of my lamps to 'soften the mood and make one's wrinkles so much less noticeable.' Another gay friend once walked into my hotel room, where I was camped out producing a show, carrying four huge glass vases and four boxes of amber and pink miniature Christmas tree lights. He strode in and, without explanation, plugged in the light sets, swirled each into the glass vases in a random pattern, and placed them around the room. OK, so I'll admit it looked gorgeous and cast a hypnotic glow. But who puts mini-lights in a vase? I'll tell you who — the same people who select napkin rings as carefully as others select engagement rings, who actually *make* potpourri, and who think aromatherapy should be tax-deductible as a medical expense."

Acknowledging that there can be too much of a good thing, the question remains: why do so many gay men share this concern for aesthetics, and indeed, share it to such an extent that it forms the cornerstone of many of their friendships with women? Certainly without this aestheticism, gay men would be largely unwilling to share in much of what they do with their women friends — spending afternoons shopping for just the perfect pillow for that new couch — not too big, not too small, not too peach, not too pink; doing dinner at the latest place downtown before attending the Antonioni retrospective sponsored by the film institute; making sure that they have tickets for the new production of Turandot at the opera, designed by David Hockney and costumed by Christian DelaCroix. Gay men share these joys, pleasures, and enthusiasms with their female friends. They live out this rich dedication to the sensual in their lives. They seem to possess a consciousness of the entire universe to be found in colors, textures, shades and flavors. Who let gay men in on this "women's" secret?

First, perhaps, we should say that the stereotype of gay men as aesthetically attuned is often just that. We must lovingly confess that we each have several gay friends with appallingly bad taste in clothes, whose interior design skills peaked with the orange crates and shag carpeting of the 70's, and who think "mohair" is what happens when you don't shave in the morning. Moreover, many gay men bristle at being treated as if they are all frustrated interior decorators and truly resent the stereotype that they are all interested in fashion and fabric swatches. Needless to say, many a woman has little or no interest in such frippery either. Laura clearly has her limits and still shudders when she recalls one endless car ride from New York to New Jersey during which two of her otherwise interesting gay friends droned on for hours about the difference between a ramekin and a crème brûlée dish. For all these caveats, however, it cannot be denied that in the worlds of theatre, fashion, decor, and the arts, gay men and straight women come together in force and in friendship.

Superficiality Runs Deep

The overwhelming presence of gay men in the arts has been a cause for endless speculation: are gay men born with an innate taste for opera, Hepplewhite antiques, and show tunes, or are gay men drawn to such pursuits and interests because of the impact of identifiable social and cultural influences?

The "explanation" of why gay men are different is a spiritual belief; a matter of personal faith rather than something objectively provable.

Different cultures have had different perspectives on this question of nature versus nurture. Some hold that gay men are of an essentially different nature than other men, a notion sometimes referred to as "essentialism." Native American tribes, for example, sometimes had an additional gender or two, beyond merely "man" and "woman," to describe people whose anatomy seemed to be combined with important spiritual, social, or emotional characteristics of the other gender. These "men-women," therefore, would be anatomical males who behaved socially like women, involving themselves in female activities and pairing with men as partners. Many tribes accepted such "men-women" because of their deep belief that these individuals were called to be this way by the Great Spirit. We might simply call such people "gay" using our own cultural lenses, but within these native cultures, these "men-women" were understood to be who they were because of an essential difference in their soul or spirit. Thus, if we borrow this attitude from native peoples, the reason that gay men share this archetypal feminine concern with beauty is because of an essential difference in their souls as men.

This persuasive argument for an "essential difference" in gay men certainly has the ring of truth to it. Many gay men will say frankly that they have always known that they were not like the other boys.

Ultimately, however, is such an "essential difference" provable? In all probability, no. Like the explanation put forward by the native Americans as an explanation for why these people inhabit the earth, the "explanation" of why gay men are different is less of an explanation and more of a spiritual belief, a matter of personal faith rather than something objectively provable. While our own culture tries to prove this "essentialist" position on homosexuality by way of genetic research, where attempts are being made to identify a "gay gene," such efforts are being met with some controversy and ridicule: is it likely that these researchers will find a gene that predisposes one to recognizing the difference between a ramekin and a crème brûlée dish? Certainly not among some of our aesthetically-challenged friends, and so, a resounding "no" can be the only answer to this genetic inquiry. Yet, the idea that gay men are somehow fundamentally different persists, and perhaps as a personal belief, as part of a person's own individual story, it should be greeted with appropriate respect.

Alongside the notion of essentialism, another explanation has been put forward as to why gay men in general seem to be so much more attuned to the aesthetic level of everyday life, to the point that many make the arts their very life and livelihood. This explanation, which one might call "social-developmental" or "constructivist" looks at the particular situation in which most gay men grow up. Being told from the outset, directly and indirectly, that they should be someone they aren't; finding out who and what they are and then realizing very early on that, to survive and be accepted, they need to hide this identity from others and pretend to be someone they aren't; honing this capacity for dissembling over many years into a fine art, making a virtue of a necessity, so to speak — all these factors eventually come to mean that a central theme in the lives of gay men is this difference between appearance and reality, between what something seems to be and what it is. When we look at gay men's development in this light, we should hardly be surprised to find that large numbers of such men, groomed by these special conditions of growing up gay in a heterosexual society, would in fact gravitate to the fields of theatre, film, decorating, fashion design, and cosmetology, fields in which appearance is reality.

Rob explains it this way: "Most gay men have become masters of aesthetic manipulation, for the developmental stakes have always been high for us. If we failed to 'pass,' as straight, if we failed to adjust our natural walk and talk in such a way so as to occasion no comment, if we did not attend in minute detail to what we wore and how we wore it, for many of us it would have been quite literally a matter of life and death. No wonder we are such entertainers! No wonder we can do wonders with costumes! No wonder we take it all — the drag, the actors, the hair, the feathers, the sightlines, the position of the hand — so very seriously."

Take your pick, for these are the two currently competing positions in gay discussions these days: essentialism (gay men are born different) versus constructivism (gay men turn out to be different due to the social conditions that shape them). In either case, as far as we are concerned, the result is identical, and this is even more true for gay men who have managed to come out. Once a gay man has realized that conventional standards of heterosexual masculinity do not and cannot apply to him, he casts such standards off and lets himself be the individual he is rather than a "man" *per se*. Thus, gay men more than most men have acquired a great appreciation for the delicious irony of appearance-versus-reality, or, in other words, their superficiality runs very deep. Gay men tend to delight in the surfaces — they do not shrink from the sensual.

This unconventional masculinity, we think, this comfort with the feminine, provides a key point of contact with women who figured out long ago the joys of being feminine and who revel in the search for the pleasing and beautiful. As Laura describes it: "Most women I know really enjoy, at least on some level, feeling feminine and beautiful. There is something wonderfully indulgent about getting a French manicure, lounging in a lavender-scented bath, or wearing something no man (except Rob, of course, who looks fabulous in feathers) could carry off. OK, so I have now made myself sound like the world's biggest bimbo. But I think the truth is, for many women, that whenever we indulge our purely feminine side, we are really connecting to a tremendous source of power. And no one appreciates this aspect of women more than gay men, who seem uniquely attuned to a woman's aesthetic side and who can admire and enjoy her femininity. This was brought home recently when Gwyneth Paltrow wore a gorgeous, very pink, dress to the Oscars. More than one gay friend remarked to me on her choice of the color — how bold, how feminine, how it said, 'I am a beautiful young woman. Deal with it.' And their attitude toward her was 'You go, girl!'"

Ironically, this one conventional aspect of the many dimensions of a woman, with its emphasis on beauty and femininity, can combine with a gay man's unconventional masculinity to form the essential basis for a wonderful friendship. Or, to say it another way, when we do the things we do together — sharing long meals in pleasant surroundings, spending leisurely afternoons in shops, going to the opening of a musical, or attending the newest exhibition downtown — straight women and gay men revel in the same things for the same reason: they're fun!

2. Talking To Each Other

Of course, the only thing better than actually *doing* something fun is getting together to *talk* about it afterward. And a gift of the gab is one blessing gay men and straight women often share in abundance. So "just getting together to talk" is on the top of just about everyone's list of things gay men

Women in general seem to regard this capacity for conversation as very unusual for a man, and it is one of the things that makes their gay male friends so important to them.

and straight women love to do together. Nearly all the women we talked with deeply appreciated their gay friends' ability to talk with them, to spend time after a movie discussing it, to meet at a cafe and chat about what is going on in each other's lives.

Women in general seem to regard this capacity for conversation as very unusual for a man, and it is one of the things that makes their gay male friends so important to them. As Karen put it, "The men I've been with, romantically speaking, mostly act either annoyed or bored when I want to sit down and talk to them about what's going on. I usually manage to get them to understand that these conversations don't need to be heavy and deep. Sometimes I just want to bounce some things off them, to get a man's point of view on whatever it is I'm thinking about. But I don't know what it is with my gay male friends — they just seem to get it. They listen, they respond — sometimes extravagantly, sometimes not — but they always respond. It's so refreshing to talk so easily and naturally to a man."

The ability and willingness to talk with one another often shows up early in relationships between gay men and straight women. Ann, talking about her initial meeting with Brad, said, "One of the things I liked the most about Brad right off was how verbal he was. I've always liked verbal guys anyway, and when I met him in the course of the film festival, I remember saying to myself how much I liked how bright and verbal he was."

Darcy echoed Ann's sentiments when talking about her gay male friends with whom she would regularly get together for Sunday morning brunch. "There was a wittiness at those brunches — jokes, comments, insults, references to movies, flying here and there. I could barely keep up half of the time and the other half of the time I didn't know what they were even referring to. But it was really great. Here they were, all men, and articulate and intelligent and quick. They were very different from the men I grew up with, Gary Cooper, mid-western, silent types. Nice guys, but you never knew what was going on inside. These gay men, who became kind of like my second family, were the best of both worlds — very male but also very vocal about their feelings and their thoughts."

And gay men we spoke with expressed a similar delight in their ability to talk to their women friends so freely. Rob's friend Lowell is quite insistent, in fact, when he says, "Actually, there are situations which I would *only* discuss with one of my woman friends. I don't know if I am burdening them or perhaps putting them in an awkward position, but I know when my partner has done something that really pisses me off, I reach right for that phone and call a girlfriend and I just know I'm going to get supported." He laughs some when he thinks about the irony of it. "I know it's a little odd to be a man complaining to women about how horrible men are, but that is what I love the most about my women friends."

Sharing thoughts and feelings can also lead to the sharing of secrets. Cynthia, who experienced great delight in sharing secrets with her gay friend, said, "One of my gay friends, with whom I've traveled some, started one day to trade secrets with me about various love affairs we had had. It was like being little kids, you know, 'I've told you one, now you tell me one.' It was fun. I don't know if I could do that sort of thing with a straight man."

And this delight in secrets goes in both directions in these friendships. When Laura asked Rob over dinner once what was special about his friendships with women, after a moment's thought, he smiled. "To tell the truth, there are things about me that only my women friends know and that really I only feel completely comfortable sharing with them. Aspects of my spiritual life, weird psychic experiences I have had, certain ideas I have had for stories or books. My partner and my male friends in general tend to be very rational and down-to-earth, so a lot of times this odd sort of stuff — intuitions, visions, fantasies and so forth — I turn to my women friends exclusively to talk about and work through. I'll often joke with my partner that there are things about me he can't even guess at, and I'm thinking of these parts of myself which are like my little secrets with my women friends."

What makes this kind of conversation between men and women possible? Are gay men more verbal, more self-expressive, brighter and wittier? Certainly one stereotype of gay men — the arch, droll bitchy queen presiding with ruthless wit over dinner parties and salons — would suggest so. And — truth be told — many gay men are indeed not too different from the stereotype. For example, Rob's friend Ron could recite the entire script of both *All About Eve* and *The Women* line for line, and did so over many a memorable evening, to the delight of those of us lounging about after dinner (though he never quite did get Marjorie Main down to a tee, God bless him — too butch, I think).

Or is it that women are in fact more naturally nurturing, talking to comfort, soothe and support as mothers, lovers, and friends? Certainly, many of the gay men we spoke with felt that way about their conversations with their female friends, knowing that they could count on a kind word and a loving connection at the other end of the phone or across the kitchen table.

Using words to establish an emotional connection, to throw a perspective on things, to make things fun or light or deep, is among the most valuable parts of the friendship between straight women and gay men. Conventional masculinity equates strength with silence, manhood with stoicism, but unconventional men can, like women, seize the great gift of language and use it as a tool to forge relationships.

Still, when it comes to the question of which gender is the most verbal, we crash solidly into a knot of conflicting stereotypes. Men hold forth publicly and in great pomp and circumstance in forums like the Senate or on TV, their words carrying authority, presence, and power. Yet it is women who buy the majority of books in this country and who define the very essence of the "talk show." Some might claim that women are rarely heard or listened to in this culture in which the media is dominated and controlled by men, and yet it is toward the female sector of the audience that the commercial media gears its products, shows and commercials. Men would say that women talk a great deal but do not say very much, while women, in turn, would probably accuse most men of saying a lot but being largely unable to simply talk to them. Even Deborah Tannen's now well-known observation that men communicate information whereas women communicate to establish emotional connection seems to indicate that neither gender is in reality *more* verbal than the other, just that women and men use verbal expression for different (and sometimes at cross) purposes.[1]

Speaking Freely

What we believe women are saying when they speak of their gay male friends' devotion to the great art of conversation is not that gay men are more verbal, but rather that gay men seem to share both an ability to communicate emotionally and a greater capacity to listen than some of their straight counterparts. Undoubtedly, part of this ease with each other comes from the lack of sexual interaction between gay men and straight women, which once again is valued as much by the gay men in these friendships as by the straight women we spoke with.

Without the tension and expectations of any sexual interaction, straight women and gay men are freed from having to edit or censor themselves with each other.

Alex, a great-looking gay man who is often on the receiving end of attention from both men and women, reflects on how sexual tension affects his ability to feel at ease with men and women: "With a straight guy, there is always in the back of your mind the idea that he might think either that you are coming on to him or, if not that, the idea that he thinks less of you because you are being nelly or silly or emotional. So, you censor yourself all the time. Is that internal homophobia? I don't know. And with other gay men, there is this unspoken sexual tension there all the time which can get in the way of talking, you know, from your soul: Does he think I'm hot? Do I think he's hot? Would I have sex with him? So all that is going on all the time, and so I don't always feel as open as I can with my women friends, where I know that none of that is happening. So I can tell my women friends everything — and not feel like I'm going to get laughed at or beaten up or misunderstood or whatever."

Without the tension and expectations of any sexual interaction, straight women and gay men are freed from having to edit or censor themselves with each other. Alex continues, "My women friends know what it is like to relate to men — how hard it can be, how frustrating, how pleasurable. I just take for granted that they know what I am talking about. With my straight male friends — and I have a lot of really great straight male friends — I always feel like I have to translate for them so they get it. They are always one step removed. My women friends are right there with me. They have had the same experiences, hit the same blocks, worked through the same stuff. And they give me some great advice. I love talking to them. They are the first people I go to with a problem or an issue, sometimes, even before my own boyfriend!"

Cynthia echoes Alex's comments when she describes her friend Dave. "I'd say that Dave is a very good friend of mine, because he is someone I am really able to open up to. Whether it has to do with his being gay, I don't know. It might. In general, gay men tend to be a lot more gentle. Dave is a very gentle person. He doesn't have that constant testosterone flow that other guys have. So many straight men are in a constant fight with the world, one-up-ing each other all the time. All that business gets very tiresome. So one of the things I like the most about gay men is that that sort of constant battling doesn't seem to exist. It just isn't there. Gay men are definitely men, but they have a different way of being a man, which is what I really like about Dave and about all of my gay friends."

Adam, who enjoys a small, select group of female friends, stresses the depth of these friendships. "I think a gay man and a straight woman can have a kind of emotional connection and a kind of friendship that's not possible between a straight man and a straight woman. I think the friendship aspect of it can be deeper. With the heterosexual friendship, there's always that possibility and 'if we're that good of friends, then why aren't we…?' If that factor is removed from the friendship, and you're both sort of attracted to basically the same things, and you're not a threat to each other, the friendship can be deeper."

Lily, one of Rob's friends who got to know him during a shared internship, reflects on the same set of issues. As she puts it, "I have to say one of the most wonderful things about my gay male friends is there isn't all that pretense and other junk that's so often present when you are meeting a heterosexual guy and checking each other out. Because all that posturing isn't there with gay men, you can take the friendship to a deeper level right away. You go, 'Whew! I don't have play all these games.' That is very attractive about gay men. You can just start enjoying what you have in common and not have to worry about what he is thinking or not thinking about you as a woman."

The capacity to talk and listen, to get and give emotional support, to know on a deep level what some other soul is going through and to empathize are the hallmarks of these friendships. Gay men and straight women prove that the "war of the sexes" is not an eternal pitched battle but that men and women can indeed have a deep, abiding connection.

We are the first to admit that such an observation flies in the face of the Mars-Venus[2] scenario proposed by John Gray (and others using different analogies) which suggests that men and women can *not* communicate naturally because they come from "different planets" and have, in effect, different languages. If this is true, why can straight women and gay men communicate so effortlessly?

The answer may be found in the things that get in the way of effortless communication between straight men and women. For example, one of John Gray's theories is that men are resistant to hearing a woman tell him all about her day because he fears she wants him to give her advice or even "fix" whatever problems came up. He is too busy searching for solutions to really relax and listen to her problems, and he feels put upon at having to go through the exercise (particularly if she ignores his advice). Our informal research confirmed that, at least according to some of the straight women we talked to, this theory has some basis in fact. Perhaps the ritual of solving a woman's problems is something straight men feel they must do in order to prove themselves worthy and desirable to women. Possibly it is based on the centuries-old stereotypes of females as being weaker and in need of a man's help and protection. There may also be a sort of "inherited impatience" that comes from a man watching his father, and his father's father, roll his eyes at the start of any conversation with his wife. Only very rarely does a father teach his son to listen and communicate well with the women in his life, a social skill either undervalued or often not even acknowledged by straight men.

Yet most gay men were raised by these same fathers, and they nonetheless have acquired an ability to listen that their straight counterparts often lack. Perhaps the best explanation for this is that gay men and straight women share something very basic in common: an empathy based upon shared sexual orientation — their common attraction to men. And although gay men certainly know that their female friends are sometimes looking to them for advice, they do not seem to feel — and thus do not resent feeling — the need to fix her problems. Of course, gay men may feel less responsible for their female friends in a basic way: they are not being called upon to provide food, shelter or to father her children. They are there to provide emotional support, and they may in fact be wildly protective of her, but the ultimate responsibility for her survival they place elsewhere – usually with the woman herself.

Yet there may be another explanation for gay men's capacity to be with women so easily and openly. Though hardly great theorists on homosexuality, both Freud and Jung identified homosexuality with a "mother complex," or to put it less technically, they thought that gay men might be gay because they had identified themselves primarily with their mothers psychologically. Nowadays, we are less concerned with what causes homosexuality, since the tide of opinion has moved more toward seeing all sexual orientation as a natural variation along a continuum. However, the core of these analytic theories concerning gay men's close affinity to their mothers finds support in the stories quoted above: gay men and women, in a certain way, share the same sexual orientation — both are attracted to men — and from this basic similarity comes an ease of relationship and an openness of experience.

Speaking from his own experience, Rob says, "From a very early age, most gay men realize that they share their interest with women rather than other men. We realize that our feelings for our fathers resemble our mother's and our sisters' feelings. First memories tend to be emblematic and so my first memory of my father is telling: a wonderful tender experience of being held close to his chest in a pool during a vacation, feeling his skin and knowing I was safe, with my mother looking on. When we gay men hear sappy love songs on the radio, it is the female part we sing along to, because it is women who express our own feelings about loving, losing and desiring men: Diana Ross, Melissa Manchester, and Bette Midler were the voice of my teenage erotic longings — and not Rod Stewart, Mick Jagger or Kenny Loggins. We develop crushes on our teachers, coaches, and family friends and, though we may never speak of them to anyone, we know that these crushes of ours are like our little girlfriend's crushes. I fell head over heels in love for the first time with my seventh grade English teacher, hanging around class afterward, wanting to hear all about his personal life, the only boy in a throng of girls who felt the same way about him."

Laura, not to be outdone on the psychology of pop tunes, counters with her own perspective. "OK, so now Rob has me worried that I must be a straight man trapped in a women's body, because I have never *once* wanted to sing along with some sappy song by Melissa Manchester. Seriously, though, I was raised by strong women without a father at home, so I tend to be one of those Venus-wannabe-but-really-just-a-pushy-Mars type women John Gray often worries about. I haven't really felt, consciously anyway, an affinity to my gay friends based on our shared attraction to men. We are simply attracted to too different a subspecies of the generic species: Male, Single, Unfathomable. But I do identify with Rob's theory about gay men's identification with their mothers, and in fact, I am often put in the mother role with some of my gay friends. With one of them in particular, I spend so much time fussing over him and pampering him, I expect any day now to start cutting his meat at the dinner table."

Whether or not there is some deep dark archetypal identification with the Feminine in gay men, what is most certainly true is that developmentally gay men know women and girls are attracted to men the way they are, and so from an early age, feel an affinity to girls and to the women they become. Gay men share their sexual orientation with women, and what's more, they *know* that they do, making their female friends the people they naturally, spontaneously turn to with their emotional lives, conflicts, and joys.

Rather than exalt gay men as more verbal and more emotionally available than straight men, as so many of the people we talked to did, perhaps we should say instead that gay men and straight women are more verbal and more emotionally available to each other than either group feels able to be with their romantic and sexual partners. This may be what, after all, distinguishes a friendship from a romantic relationship and makes our friends at least as important to most of us as our lovers, partners and spouses.

Ten Great Lies

However, we would like to suggest with an evil gleam in our co-authorial eyes that there is one more verbal skill that allows gay men and straight women to connect so deeply, an overlooked and yet extremely

Gay men and straight women know when to tell the truth, but they also know when to spruce it up a little.

significant part of nearly every one of these friendships: namely, the willingness and ability to lie convincingly, on command if necessary. Straight men often panic when they are confronted with a question like "Honey, do I look fat in this?"

Because they think it is an actual, non-rhetorical question, they find themselves bumbling and stumbling for the "right" answer. Gay men and straight women don't have to struggle: they know when to tell the truth, but they also know when to spruce it up a little – when to look their friend straight in the eye and tell them precisely whatever they want to hear.

Based on some wholly unscientific research — to wit, our own experiences — we've listed below ten of the most popular lies gay men and straight women tell each other. Though we are sure that our readers could supply many more, here goes our list, with appropriate stage directions provided:

1. He just wasn't good enough for you.

This lie works best after a couple of cocktails, but to be fully effective you cannot let your friend go on any longer than ten minutes about how he or she was at fault for being dumped. You grasp your friend's hand firmly and deliver this fib with complete earnestness to end this "foolish talk" abruptly, following up with "You're too complex a person to settle for just anyone, you know."

2. *That outfit makes you look much thinner.*

   This lie requires that you scrutinize your friend's entire body no less than twice, ending up with an unflinching gaze and half-smile full in the face. The key to delivering this line is the subtle half-smile, as if you have seen something very pleasing but don't want to embarrass your friend by gushing too much about how much weight he or she has lost. It also works to appear worried, making the concerned inquiry: "Are you eating?"

3. *Gray hair is becoming on you.*

   This lie is difficult to carry off, so you might try outright denial instead: "It's not gray, silly, it's platinum!" Alternatively, you might counsel acceptance. To quote a greeting card we saw recently: "It's time to come out of the closet: you're gray!"

4. *That simply can't be your correct age.*

   One technique that will make this particular lie go down easily is to laugh uncomfortably, as if at your own stupidity, hand at the throat, eyes wide in disbelief. Here is one place where overplaying your incredulity will work wonders.

5. *No one noticed that you had too much to drink last night.*

Do not hand your friend aspirin, ice pack or raw egg concoctions while saying this, if you wish to be believed. Follow it up with a compliment, like: "everyone just thought you were vivacious!"

6. *Those aren't wrinkles — they are laugh lines.*

Exhibit your own laugh lines with a ridiculous grimace if you want your friend to swallow this bit of friendly deceit. Or wave your hand dismissively while declaring, "So what are you supposed to do? Frown your whole life?" Or you can put your nose up in the air and opt for the high road: "My attitude is, I've earned every line on my face."

7. *Yes, your entire family is crazy; you are the normal one.*

Allowing your friend to go on at extraordinary lengths about his or her insane relatives before responding with the above will help immensely. Even if you think everything you've heard about his father or her mother sounds suspiciously familiar, whatever you do, don't smirk or roll your eyes.

8. *You are so much better looking than his new love interest.*

   Okay, she was stunning, he was a hunk to die for. Everyone at the whole party beat a path to them, your friend's ex gloated disgustingly the whole evening, and you and your friend ended up eating way too many miniature quiches in the corner. You aren't going to be believed no matter what you say. So say this polite lie with a minimum of fuss and quickly change the subject.

9. *That was delicious, whatever it was. Can I have the recipe?*

   It goes without saying that you have to have eaten all of "whatever it was" to have a prayer of being taken for sincere when saying this. But try not to make a face when you get the recipe and find out that the secret ingredient was something you are allergic to.

   And on occasion, a straight woman is required to state, unequivocally:

10. *No, you are not all that obviously gay.*

    Variations on this particular lie include: "No, you are not a huge screaming queen," "Yes, I find you incredibly attractive as a man," and "Really, now, can there be such a thing as too much hair mousse?" Based on insecurity, the gay man who needs this lie also probably needs a hug or a kiss on the cheek, too. Supply both with abundance.

What we are saying here, in a not-too-serious way, is a little white lie between friends is OK. But there comes a time in these friendships when only the truth will do.

3. Coming Out as the Moment of Truth

 In every friendship, there is a moment of truth when two friends confront each other with the reality

To gay men, coming out is one of the most important events in their lives.

of who they really are, each seeking the understanding and acceptance of the other. In many of the friendships between gay men and straight women, this moment of truth occurs when the man "comes out" and first announces to his female friend that he is gay. How she reacts can either bring their friendship to an abrupt end, or more frequently, can form the essential building block in the foundation of a lifelong relationship between them.

The phrase "coming out" has long meant different things to men and women. To women, it can mean a charming tradition where a young woman is first presented to society, or it can mean a hellish evening when a girl is forced to wear a hideous white dress, pretend to be a virgin, and dance with the pimply-faced son of her parents' golfing partners. To gay men, however, coming out is one of the most important events in their lives.

Begin at the Beginning

One cannot really overestimate the significance of the coming-out process in the life of a gay man: it is a starting point and an ending point, and in many ways, it represents nothing less than the

At a young age, when these young gay men don't fit in with the other boys, they often turn to girls for friendship.

birth of his personality. For this reason, coming out, as a moment, as a process, and as a turning point in a gay man's development, figures so prominently in the life stories of gay men. As we found during our interviews, if you ask a gay man to talk about any aspect of his life, including his friendships with women, the story will nearly always begin with a coming-out story — how and when he realized he was gay, and then, what effect that realization had psychologically and socially on his life and on his relationships with his family, and, of course, with his friends.

The momentous quality of this realization is easy to understand given what a gay man is up against in his development. Typically born into families that by definition came into existence through a heterosexual relationship, gay men grow up in a social and cultural world almost always devoid of encouragement, support, or even awareness of homosexuality. And that is in the best of cases. Worse still are those familial and social environments in which homosexuality is used as a symbol for everything bad, evil and dirty, where the young gay man is bombarded with messages that he is essentially sinful. From the family at home, where homosexuality may be a matter of indifference at best or the focus of intense hatred at worst, the developing gay man then goes to school where the vast majority of his peers are heterosexual, where the social fabric of his teachers' lives present a nearly unremittingly heterosexual face, and where the history, literature and cultural norms he is taught in class are again centered on heterosexual relationships.

If the young man is lucky, he may find a kindred soul in a classmate or two or may be accurately seen and mirrored by an unusually perceptive teacher. Yet even these potentially positive experiences can be fraught with negative aspects. He and his friend may be joined together in their own (and in other's minds) because they are the two class misfits, the weirdos, the guys who can't throw a ball, the ones no one wants on their team. And it is an exceedingly rare educational environment in which gay teachers feel entirely at ease sharing themselves freely with their young male pupils. So young gay men hit puberty in nearly complete psychological, social and cultural isolation when it comes to sexuality, sometimes fortunate to have some idea that there are other men like them but mostly feeling as if they are "the only one in the world."

Nevertheless, the seeds for friendships between gay men and straight women are often sown at this time in the early relationships between a boy and a sensitive female teacher, who may understand and nurture his uniqueness and creativity but who, sadly, cannot address issues of sexual confusion and curiosity. At a young age, when these young gay men don't fit in with the other boys, they often turn to girls for friendship. Being the last two people picked for dodgeball can form the basis for a lasting friendship. And since many prepubescent boys express their affection by spitting on and otherwise physically and emotionally terrorizing the young girls of their dreams, many girls are happy to turn to a young boy who is kinder, gentler, and who does not appear likely to inflict imminent bodily harm. Laura remembers fondly a friend who played dolls with her (he called them action figures), and her Barbie and his GI Joe shared quite a romance until Malibu Ken arrived. This childhood friend of hers is now a gay florist in Los Angeles and, interestingly, is dating someone who looks quite a bit like Malibu Ken.

Young girls often develop their first "crush" on boys who have an essential sweetness, softness, even a feminine quality. Today young girls are attracted to Leonardo DiCaprio and the Hansens, performers who are the antithesis of dangerous or intimidating, men who come off as slightly androgynous or even unformed sexually. Young girls are often drawn to boys who are classically beautiful in a smooth, lithe, and hairless way, and this pattern of androgynous attraction on the part of such girls may represent a sort of compromise or midway point: ready to transfer her sexual interests away from her father, who up to now has been the most important man in her young life, she begins to become attracted to boys outside the family who are her own age. She is not yet fully ready developmentally to deal with the very alien and sometimes scary world of sexually mature adult males. Her natural choice of love object, therefore, is a boy considerably less than that — sweet and tender, rather than rough and phallic; slightly girlish and fey, rather than inarguably male and aggressive.

Adam, an actor who has traveled extensively in Asia, noted this phenomenon there. "In Japan, it's really common for teenage girl comic books, which feature the usual schoolgirl adventure, to include one story which is obviously a love story between two men. I saw one where two men with 'western' features, wearing some knights-of-the-round-table type outfits with ruffled sleeves, were shown embracing, kissing, and obviously being physically intimate. I showed this to my Japanese friend and asked: 'What's the deal with these two men?' He said, 'Oh yeah, it's absolutely not threatening to these young Japanese women on any level who are seeking romance. It's so removed from them that there's no threat from the love between men in this story whatsoever. It's the safest possible form of sexual, romantic expression.'" Given this common pattern of attraction to "softer" young men, it is not surprising that so many women report that their first crush or even their first boyfriend turned out to be gay.

As they progress through junior high and high school, young gay men and straight women often come together in some fairly stereotypical places: the drama club, cheerleading, art class, and other places where they can find expression for their creative impulses. Sometimes, though, they meet as misfits with an attitude, smoking behind the gym, joining a rock band, and challenging authority whenever possible. They may date each other as the young gay man comes to terms with his sexuality and as the young woman turns to someone who feel safer and more comfortable for her first experiences with men. When this happens, the young man struggling to come out is put in a very special bind, for he must not only risk the potential negative reaction of society, his family and his friends but must also risk losing the friendship of a young woman who has become dear to him.

Given all these pressures, the lack of support, the dearth of understanding, the awful risk of rejection, that gay men come out at all has a near miraculous quality to it, and some of this quality is sensed when you hear a gay man's coming out story. It sounds like a conversion experience, a return from exile, an expansion of consciousness, the answer to an existential riddle, and a gay man's own individual personal, social and cultural revolution — all wrapped up into a single momentous step forward. And for many a gay man, his female friends were with him when it happened.

Let Me Tell You Something

It appears that a female friend is, more often than not, the first person to whom a gay man says, "I'm gay." Through all our conversations for this book, gay men told us time and time again that their straight female friends were among the first people they had come out to. They were the people gay men felt most confident would understand and accept them unconditionally.

Rob's experience was as follows. "The first person I had ever said I was gay to was my friend Sasha in college. It was during my sophomore year at Georgetown and I remember the moment clearly, though it's now 20 years ago. Throughout high school, I had had three notable 'unrequited love affairs' with straight friends, all of which opened my eyes to my own nature, and, being helped a great deal by growing up close to New York, I arrived at school on the cusp of finally "coming out." What I lacked then was the language: I knew what I had felt for the men I had fallen in love with in high school, and I knew my feelings for them were far more absorbing than what I had felt for the two girls I had dated — far more absorbing by a power of about a thousand. And yet, what was it? What was I? I was definitely different, but at that time, what that difference was called I did not yet know.

"Sasha, I'm sure, even today, does not suspect the role she played in my coming out, but it was

Gay men told us time and time again that their straight female friends were among the first people they had come out to.

through her participation in the gymnastics team, some of whose members lived in my sophomore dorm and whose relationships with each other were whispered about, that all the pieces clicked into place.

"'You know, those two at the end of the hall,' my roommate that year said to me one day. 'Yeah?' said I, studying at my desk. He said, 'They're gay, you know.'

"Gay. I thought a bit. Of course. I had heard the word, but it conjured up visions of some of the more effeminate teachers in my high school, fussy older men, no one I could identify with. And yet, the two guys at the end of the hall — well-built jocks, wicked senses of humor, meticulous about their clothes, friends of Sasha. Oh . . . *that* was it! Click. I was gay. I had heard through her and her friends that these two rarely socialized on campus but would go out dancing down in Dupont Circle. Click. Dupont Circle. Gay men. Click. *That* was it. That's what I was. That was what had been going on with my crushes in high school.

"I marched down the hall, knocked on her door, sat down on Sasha's bed and said, 'You know what? I'm gay.' She looked at me strangely but without judgment. 'You know I thought so, but I wasn't sure. I was confused,' she replied. 'Confused?' I asked.

"She just continued to look at me, and then I remembered, what had happened not even three months before. We had come back to school after Christmas vacation and full of post-adolescent hormones in need of expression, Sasha and I ended up making out together, a quick and furtive release for both of us, for the first and only time in our friendship. But typically, we didn't need to say a whole lot, capable as good friends are of reading each other's minds.

"'I couldn't figure it out,' Sasha said. 'I just assumed you were gay, given the way you talk about your friend back home, but then you just kind of threw yourself at me. It was confusing.'

"I felt a whole range of feelings at once thinking about how she had responded to me that afternoon, how she was responding to me now — understanding, accepting, compassionate — even though in my own unconsciousness, I had in a way used her. I felt ashamed. I felt loved. I felt relieved. I felt free.

"'I guess I was horny,' was about the only thing I could get out, being the sheepish post-adolescent that I was at the time. She laughed. 'Hey, it was OK by me. Me, too. It happens.'

"I loved her so much at that moment. She was so great. None of that 'girlie' stuff — the guilt-tripping, the woundedness, no "how could you" or "you lied to me" or "why don't you like me?" Just the same kind of even-tempered, matter-of-fact constant friendship.

"She smiled. 'I won't tell anyone. You planning to tell your parents?' I paused and then replied, 'Haven't thought about it. Probably not for a while.' At that we both rolled our eyes, in tacit agreement at the effect that would have. 'Our secret then,' she said, kissing me on the cheek. 'Guess so,' I said, relaxing. "For now."

"And so it stayed, a secret between Sasha and me. It made so much difference to have my own coming to consciousness greeted without condemnation, tears, or fears. It set the stage for the subsequent comings-out, so to speak — to other friends later that year and the next year, in Italy, and then eventually to my own family and to the larger community of Georgetown during my political activities in my senior year. My friendship with Sasha played a vital role in making me who I am, in giving me a place to go with my knowledge of who I was that was loving, understanding, open and safe."

Unlike Sasha, not all female friends are instantly accepting, but many come around eventually. Adam, who grew up in a small, conservative western town, tells the story of one of his best friends from high school. "She was very popular, student body president and all that. I think maybe there was a time when she had stronger feelings for me than I did for her, but we were such good friends that we got over that. We've had really long, intimate talks. In those days, I was trying really hard not to be a homosexual, because I didn't want to be. When I came out, it was tough, because when I decided to tell her, she was going through a revivalist, 'Jesus-freak' stage. It didn't go well, and we separated for a few years after that. She thought it was a sin and that I was sinning. But she got over that, and now we're great friends."

Timing can be everything. Joey, a young actor, told us his story. He began, "My girlfriend was married to a very prominent man in town, a very small southern town. I really thought I was straight and I thought that she was 'it.' I still have such strong feelings for her, she was my soul mate — we always thought that. Eventually her husband found out about the affair, the whole town found out, and my parents found out. We literally got caught with our pants down. We broke up, and I moved to another city. She stayed in our home town but divorced her husband."

Unfortunately, Joey chose the wrong moment to tell his ex-girlfriend he was gay. Continuing with his story, he said, "The night that I told her I was gay, I had gone home to see her in our small town. We went to this bar where we used to go when we were dating, and she had already started seeing the guy she is married to now. That man, whom she eventually married, was in the bar that night with someone else. And so there she was, seeing him with somebody else while I was sitting there telling her I was gay. She flipped out. She was so mean to me that night. After being my biggest supporter, she said 'I can't deal with this tonight,' and she left. I was absolutely crushed because I thought she was the one person who was going to get me through this, but she turned and ran. But it only took her a week to call me back and apologize."

When women have a less-than-favorable immediate reaction to a friend's coming out, this often has less to do with the gay man than with something else going on, or not going on, in a woman's life. Candace admitted, "There was a time when a number of my friends, whom I hadn't even suspected were gay, all came out within a short period of time. And while I was happy for them and tried to be supportive, I'll admit that I had some negative feelings about it. It was as if a steady stream of the smartest, brightest, most attractive men I knew had all rejected women and decided that they preferred men. And after about the third or fourth time, you think: 'Is everybody gay? Is there anyone out there who still prefers women?' Those feelings don't last, of course, because you quickly realize that these men were not rejecting women, and that there would never have been a real possibility of romance with these men anyway. So you become grateful for their honesty and the friendship can grow stronger as a result."

No, Let Me Tell *You* Something

Some women friends seemed to know that their friend was gay even before he was aware of it. The issue then becomes, should she raise it with him, or let him discover it in his own time? Cathie and Matt, lifelong friends and talented performers who are now both working on Broadway, managed to achieve that delicate balance. Matt describes Cathie's sensitive way of handling his reluctance to come out. "It got to a point where she knew, and everyone knew, but I hadn't admitted it. It was great because no one forced me. No one said, 'We've figured this out, your male friend is always

A gay man's female friend may be more than a sympathetic observer of his coming out process; she may be an instigator and proponent.

at your house, and you're not dating any women.' No one 'outed' me. A good friend lets you have that space. It was one little aspect of our friendship we hadn't talked about, and we knew it would come out eventually — or at least Cathie knew. I can't stand outing. In a perfect world, everybody could be who they are and who they want to be, and no one would have any problem with it. But unfortunately we're human beings, and it's not a perfect world. Everyone has their own issues, their own time frame, and their own journey. I thank God for Cathie because she was so supportive."

Cathie had definite feelings about this delicate issue. She explains her approach this way: "The year before Matt came out, people would call me and ask, 'Is Matt gay? Come on, he's got to be gay.' I'd say, 'He probably is, but he hasn't told me.' That's the hard thing: there's a difference between knowing and being ready to embrace it. That's why I think 'outing' is a terrible thing. I don't think it's constructive, and it could damage the relationship. I mean if you're in private and the question comes up you can ask, but I never felt the need to."

Matt later reflected upon how well his friend Cathie had handled his coming out. He remembers, "My friends all accepted it, especially my girl-friends, including Cathie. Of course, with people in show business, they're fine. But Cathie was especially terrific about it. She said she loved the guy I had fallen in love with. I think they were all waiting for me to accept it. And what I love about them is that no one said a thing about it to pressure me into it or out of it. They let me do it on my own terms and on my own timetable. That was the right approach for me, because I was very, very afraid, although there was nothing to be afraid of. I was afraid peo-ple wouldn't include me, that it wouldn't be the same — but it's better, because I'm an open book. There's nothing to hide; there are no secrets people can hold over my head. And Cathie's support was really helpful in making that happen."

Sometimes, though, the straight woman in a gay man's life is actually his girlfriend or lover, and if she becomes aware of his homosexuality before he is willing to admit it to himself, her awareness can certainly propel his coming out process. Patrick, who was then living in a quiet town in the West, had a series of affairs with women despite his feeling he was gay. Then, one woman changed his mind. Patrick recalls, "When I was first coming out, I came out long before I had sex with a man. I was still sleeping with women. All the women I was involved with were wonderful women, and one woman sort of broke the spell. We had spent the night together. The next morning I woke up and was sitting up in bed looking out the window when I thought she was asleep. And she said, 'You're never going to find *him* looking out the window.'"

Joey, the soft-spoken young man who moved from his small hometown to New York to become an actor, first heard the suggestion that he was gay from the older, wiser married woman with whom he was having an affair. Joey recalls, "She was older than I was when we first started seeing each other; I was late teens and she was late twenties. She is an artist, and she's very aware of gay men and has a lot of gay friends. When we were dating, she used to say 'I think you're gay and I want you to know that I love you no matter what and there's nothing you could do that would make me not love you. I want you to enjoy it and not be ashamed of it.'" Joey paused, and then added, "I would get sort of offended, because I was trying to fight it so much. But her saying that I was gay started me thinking: 'Why does she think that? Why does everybody think that?' I just couldn't identify with anybody I knew who was gay, so I kept saying 'No, I'm not that way.' What I really felt was that I just hadn't met the right girl. I definitely don't think that any more."

As these stories illustrate, a gay man's female friend may be more than a sympathetic observer of his coming out process; she may be an instigator and proponent. And he may well be more open to hearing the suggestion that he is gay from a woman than from any of his male friends. These female friends are therefore uniquely positioned in the lives of their gay friends to help them come to an awareness of themselves and to provide support for their coming out.

Bridges to the Past

Many of the friendships between gay men and straight women date back to childhood and to the towns where these friends grew up together. Indeed, when Bob first came out to his childhood friend Margaret, they were both in their twenties and were assumed by everyone to be romantically involved. The first reaction of Bob's parents upon hearing the news of his homosexuality was: "But who is going to marry Margaret?"

When a gay man comes out to a lifelong friend, someone he has grown up with, he is often coming out to his entire hometown.

Even after we move away, childhood friends are often a link to those back home. Joey says, "I have a number of close female friends, including one I've known since I was a child who I've kept in touch with over the years. It took me a while after I was 'out' to tell my childhood friend I was gay. She was still living in the small town where we grew up, and I didn't see her that much, but we talked on the phone a lot. People at home always ask her if I'm straight or gay, and she's very protective about it.

She says, 'I don't know, you'll have to ask him.' She doesn't want to be the one to tell them. As of this year, I've told her, 'I don't give a damn, tell them yes, tell them it's great, tell them whatever.'"

As we've seen, when a gay man comes out to a lifelong friend, someone he has grown up with, he is often coming out to his entire hometown. Patrick, who had been persuaded to come out by a female lover, ultimately came out to his small town community to avoid hurting Lisa, his closest female friend. He told us, "I was so in love with the first man I had ever fallen in love with, but he was straight. So I thought, well, my high school girlfriend had always been in love with me, and if I can't have this man, then at least somebody ought to be happy — so I decided to marry her. But then I saw another man I was attracted to and realized it would be a mistake. I broke off my relationship with Lisa, which was really hard because we were from the same small town. I had to tell her, then tell my parents, and tell her parents. At this point, the wedding dress was made, we were within inches of the wedding. I didn't want it to look like I dumped her, so I went to her father and said, 'I'm breaking it off because I'm gay; it's not Lisa, it's me, and I don't want anyone thinking it is, so you are perfectly welcome to tell anyone in this town.' And that's what Lisa's mother did: she told everyone in town that I was gay."

Ingrid's life-long friendship with Kenneth began, similarly, in their hometown. Ingrid recalls, "Kenneth is ten years older than I am, and we met when I was a teenager, because he played with my father's orchestra. I didn't know him as well as my parents did, of course, but I was aware of him as someone who came and went from our apartment. He was a fabulous piano player, and he organized the musical aspects of a play my school did on Louis XVI and Marie Antoinette. He even got my little brother and sister to sing in French. So he was part of that whole show-business world that was very exciting to me at that point. I knew he was different even then. He was a very shiny person, bright, quite unlike some of the dull blades in my hometown, and I really liked that brilliance he had a lot."

Ingrid paused, then continued, "Kenneth turned up again in my life about thirty years later when he applied for a faculty position at the music conservatory where I was teaching. He had by that time gotten out of performing and had pursued an academic career, becoming a very respected figure in his field, though it wasn't always easy achieving this status and being a gay man. When I heard he had applied, I thought our school would be damn lucky to get someone of Kenneth's personal and professional caliber. I reconnected with him during that interview week, this wonderful person out of my past whom I remembered with such warmth. I admired his professional status, of course, but I just knew I wanted him around. I wanted to do anything I could to promise friendship because I needed him to be there. And I had a feeling of family connection to him, from my childhood. He was a trustworthy soul."

Having a friend who has known you your whole life can be invaluable when facing life's day-to-day challenges. Adam tells this story of a trusted female friend, "When I ask for guidance from a woman, it's usually about practical, life-management questions. My best female friend, a friend from high school, has two kids, and I ask her about how she balances her life. She keeps me in touch with reality because she's in the real world. She's a single mother with two kids. And when I start feeling cranky or that life is getting me down or that I have problems, I call her, because no matter what my problems are like, she has her own problems, and she just gives me a great deal of strength. We talk about how grateful we are for what we have, and because she's one of my oldest friends, we have that unique perspective of both seeing each other's dreams come true."

Jack had a friend who taught him the meaning of self-confidence. He recalls, "I first met Marcy in college. We were aware of each other in high school because I was in a rock band and she'd come to hear us play, but we weren't close. We did a show together in college and were friendly, but it wasn't until we later moved to the same city that we became really close. We've been attached at the hip ever since. I've learned a lot from her. She's a very independent, very strong person — very driven. I was raised to question myself, "Am I good enough? Maybe I need to work harder?' Marcy's not as inse-cure. She's got it, and that's what's so great about her. She has a lot of self-assurance and I've learned a lot from her about self confidence — and about sushi."

The importance of a gay man's friendships with those he has known since childhood are included in John Preston's unique collection of stories from gay men, entitled *Hometowns* in which two dozen or so gay writers were asked to meditate upon the places they came from. In his introduction, Preston notes, "The voyage of almost all these gay writers is the same. They follow, in one way or another, a basic outline. It begins with the sense of exile from the original hometown, an expulsion that was either delightful, because of the freedom it presented, or painful, because of the abandonment it stood for. The hometown of their birth was either the writer's worst nightmare or an Eden that still has its appeal. From there, the gay man moves on to his new place in the world and explores it. He is either captivated by his new experience, or horrified by the changes he must undergo to make his new world work for him."[3]

In these friendships, it seems gay men have found a way of doing what Preston describes and even going one better: not only do they move on to their new place in the world by coming out, but by maintaining their friendships with the women they grew up with, they preserve a bridge to their past as well. Similarly, what comes through for the women is the importance of their history with these men, the deep feeling of trust and family that these friendships provide. As Dorothy said at the end of

The Wizard of Oz and as these particularly life-long friendships prove, "There's no place like home."

The Big Secret

Whether a gay man's female friends stay behind in his home town or are waiting for him in the new world he seeks, the effect of his coming out may in fact be incredibly liberat-

"It was incredibly freeing that 'this' was no longer hanging over our heads."

ing for them both. Laura has enjoyed the friendship of one man for many years whom she absolutely adored "as a friend": "This man was so brilliant and funny, the consummate host, an accomplished chef and a wonderful friend. We worked together, and we had so much in common that our coworkers always made me feel guilty that he and I were not "dating," although I don't think he had that expectation either. When he and I would go places together, I would sometimes be concerned that people might misconstrue our relationship, which really was platonic. I was so sure he was straight – he was married, then divorced, and he definitely dated women.

I don't think either of us was consciously aware at the time that he was gay. It's funny, now that I know about it, because so many of the things we had in common were stereotypically "gay:" he had a collection of Broadway musicals on CD, and once he even invited me over to his house for an intimate dinner and played me his Doris Day album – a mixed message if I've ever heard one. He eventually came out and introduced me to his lover, whom I absolutely adore. When I spend time with him now, there is none of that 'are-they-dating?' pressure, and I can just experience the pure joy of his friendship. So his coming out was great for both of us."

Candace had a similar experience. She remembers, "It was incredibly freeing that 'this' was no longer hanging over our heads. We were able to share a number of things honestly once the Big Secret was out, and the intimacy of our friendship just grew exponentially from there."

Once it's all sorted out — she's straight, he's gay, and that's not going to change — the two friends can then focus on what's *really* important: the desirable guys who are the objects of their affection. Having met the challenge of coming out, and having demonstrated mutual acceptance and understanding, friends are able to be honest with one another about the men they love, and to share all the joy, pain and delicious gossip their love lives entail.

4. Playing the Field ...
   Together

As gay men and straight women tend to be more verbal and more emotionally available to one other and because they share romantic natures and a mutual appreciation for a great looking guy, it is only natural that they should spend so much of their time talking with one another about their love

> *"When we walk down the street together, a gay friend will often say, 'Oh, that guy was checking you out,' and I'll say, 'No, I think he was looking at you,' and we'll both walk away feeling better about ourselves."*

lives. Indeed, one of the qualities straight women often single out about their gay male friends is that they are not only capable of having romantic relationships, they are willing to talk about them – *endlessly*!

"See that cute guy? Does he play for your team or mine?"

The very first thing gay men and straight women often talk about is whether an attractive man encountered on the street, in line at the grocery store, or posing with a drink in his hand at a party, is straight or gay. This has been Laura's experience, when out and about with her gay friends: "When we walk down the street together, a gay friend will often say, 'Oh, that guy was checking you out,' and I'll say, 'No, I think he was looking at you,' and we'll both walk away feeling better about ourselves. We frequently divide up the staff at a restaurant or bar by which of us the cute waiter was flirting with, or spar over which one of us the cute salesperson was hitting on. Now when this happens while walking down Castro Street in San Francisco, chances are it's my friend he's looking at, but in New York, I've got a fighting chance.

Marcy's experience with her gay friends is similar to Laura's. She says, "We love to window shop on Madison Avenue and we also love to people watch on Madison Avenue. We'll see a cute boy and we'll argue for blocks which one of us he was checking out. 'He was checking me out.' 'No, he was checking me out.' It's a game we love to play!"

Of course, the fact that straight women and gay men would spend their time "cruising" together makes complete sense and provides one of the most fun aspects of their friendships. As a team, they are darn near unbeatable. No man is safe! And, if the friendship is good and solid, whatever disappointment one partner may feel in having to "hand over" a catch to the other is more than compensated for in the knowledge that one has made a friend happy — at least for the time being. As Rob explains, "I like going out with my girlfriends and checking out the guys. It's a whole different dynamic and lots more fun with women. Gay guys get so competitive, but women are very cool about it. And there is always that element of surprise, you never know what's going to happen. Is he? Isn't he? I used to do this all the time with my friend Sandy in college, hang around the neighborhood, reading the paper for hours and trying to look fetching, having spent the whole morning trying to achieve a tousled, casual look. Many times, I thought a guy was coming on to me, but he was really trying to worm his way into getting to know her, which in some ways was even more of a thrill. But then a few times there was definitely that Elizabeth Taylor, *Suddenly Last Summer* thing going on between us, particularly when we would go out to mixed gay/straight clubs to dance, and Sandy would be sort of man-bait for me. A guy would ask her to dance at a club but then sort of drag me in on the floor. It became pretty obvious he was too shy to ask me directly. God bless her, she was a good sport, but that's why we were such good friends."

Ingrid and her gay friends also have a great deal of fun sharing comments and conversation about guys they are mutually attracted to. As Ingrid puts it, "One of the ways I love relating to some of my gay church friends is talking about guys they find attractive. Sometimes the guys that they find attractive are the same guys I find attractive, even though there may be a twenty-year age difference between me and the friend I'm talking to. Still the two of us can share our opinion that Patrick Stewart is hot stuff that you can't get enough of and that he's the *only* reason we are going to the new Star Trek movie. That's one part of my friendships with gay men that I find really fun."

Of course, once these friends have spotted Prince Charming, it becomes vital to determine whether that Prince wants to put the glass slipper on Cinderella or on the cute groomsman driving her coach.

Picking Up Signals

Straight women find gay men downright invaluable when there is any doubt regarding the sexual orientation of a man they are interested in or even involved with. Women will often ask a gay friend to

"Gay men just know. I guess they've developed ways of spotting one another, but their reasoning often surprises me."

employ his "gay-dar" to clear up any confusion about a man's sexuality, even before she will seek the opinion of a girlfriend on the subject.

Laura has a number of her own "tales from the dating front": "My gay friends are always willing to speculate about whether a man I'm interested in is gay. When circumstances have called for it, they have even been willing to venture in bravely and actually find out – they are kind of like my sexual offensive linebackers. On the other hand, my girl-friends don't know whether a man is gay any more than I do. We all have our theories: Does he love showtunes? Does he know the difference between beige and taupe or lavender and mauve? Has he ever used the word 'blouse' in conversation? But for a reliable opinion, you can only turn to a gay man. Gay men just know. I guess they've developed ways of spotting one another, but their reasoning often surprises me. I'll ask, 'Is that guy gay?' And my gay friend will respond, 'He can't be. Look at that tie," or "He's too good looking in a boring, John Tesh kind of way," or "Gay men don't stand like that." In other words, their theory seems to be that if a man is sufficiently boring, poorly dressed, unimaginative or clumsy, chances are he's straight. It's annoying, of course, that this has, on occasion, turned out to be true."

Gay men agree that women should ask them whenever they're in doubt. Patrick, a former bar-tender who has heard it all, told us, "I think it's wise for straight women to ask me whether a man is gay or not. I think it's smart if they can't do it them-selves, although straight women who've hung around with gay men can usually tell for themselves.

There are too many gay men who haven't come to terms with their gayness who will use you in ways to assuage their own inner psychic turmoil. You should stay away from them at all costs. But on the other hand, I think you should run to the nearest stable gay man, because you'll never find a better friend. You'll also never be given a truer, more objective, clear-eyed view of yourself than you will from a gay man who cares about you."

Jack, a successful actor, gets asked to determine a guy's orientation all the time by women in and out of show business. He says, "If a woman works in the-atre, she usually knows if a man is gay. If he makes one reference to the Wizard of Oz, that's it — he's out of here. If one of my close friends was involved with a man I suspected of being gay but who hasn't told her, I would tell her. I just think it is wrong. It's not wrong if she knows — that's a different story — but deception is wrong. You can't have that in a rela-tionship. It is also dangerous, with AIDS and other diseases. I would worry if a bisexual man involved with my female friend sleeps with men. How careful is he? Does he do it when he is loaded? When does he do it? Is it a little itch that has to be satisfied or a definite attraction toward men?"

When advice to a female friend is insufficient to keep her away from a sexually ambivalent man, a good gay friend is prepared to take swift action. Matt tells this story about his friend Cathie's narrow escape. "There was a Christmas party at my house, and my friend Cathie had had a couple of drinks. She was in the bathroom making out with a guy who was 'previously gay' but who kept swearing that he was now straight. I had known this guy's former boyfriend, who told me that this man would go see women all the time and would have girlfriends, so maybe he truly was bisexual. But when I found out that he was in the bathroom making out with my friend, I dragged her out of there. I wanted more for her than a 'confused' man."

Matt and Cathie laugh about Matt's noble rescue to this day. But, of course, gay men sometimes turn to their straight women friends for the same service, which has been Rob's experience. "My friend Sandy's 'gay-dar' has always been loads better than mine. Half the time I would think these guys at the clubs were just being polite to me, and after three seconds, Sandy would be next to me, going, 'Rob, oh Rob, don't you two want a little time by yourself,' wink, wink, nudge, nudge. I used to think I was missing a gene or something. She always seemed to know who was interested in whom but me, I'd always be surprised. So I asked her one day, 'How do you know who's gay and who's straight?' She laughed and replied, 'Oh it's very simple. Straight guys look at my breasts. Gay men look at my makeup and hair.'

Having figured out just who is pursuing whom, each friend must chase his or her own romantic prey. But it's understood that they are expected to report back to their friends for a full debriefing and that they will receive attention, advice, and, when needed, sympathy.

For What It's Worth...

One of the most satisfying things gay men and straight women do together is to swap stories about their love lives, particularly since they know that their friend is always going to take their side. After all, what are friends for? As Alex told us, "I would talk to straight women about really close relationships before I would talk to straight men or gay men. My female friends are more relationship-oriented; it's something they want to talk about. I don't think that guys, straight or gay, really want to talk about relationships with me. I've just found that my straight female friends are the people I can talk to about that."

Similarly, Marcy said, "Whenever I tell my gay friend about my relation-

These friends often have strong feelings about their friends' boyfriends, and their "thumbs up or down" carries a great deal of weight.

ship problems, I know he'll always say, 'You're too good for him and he doesn't deserve you.'"

These friends often have strong feelings about their friends' boyfriends, and their "thumbs up or down" carries a great deal of weight. About her experience with this, Josie said, "As a woman, I know I can rely on my gay friend's opinion of my boyfriends. He knows men better than I do, and his only interest is to see me happy. With a girlfriend, there is always that worry about jealousy or competitiveness, which is not there with a gay man. And girlfriends will be impressed with the same things you are. They'll get carried away by the looks, the job, all the 'right things' he says. But a gay man can sometimes see beyond all that to the man underneath."

Equally important can be a boyfriend's reaction to a woman's gay friend. Cathie told us, "When my boyfriends would meet my gay best friend, it was a very important thing how they took to him and reacted to him. Because he is in my life, and if a boyfriend of mine was not comfortable that I have a gay friend, that is going to cause problems."

Gay men can also help women to understand what men are really thinking, without relying solely on what they might be saying. A woman will often turn to a gay man when she just can't decipher what a straight man is trying to communicate to her. Laura herself tells of employing her gay friends as translators. "I have frequently asked my gay friends to translate "guy-speak" into English. They are very helpful at breaking the code for phrases like 'Can I call you?' or 'I'm looking for a relationship,' particularly when a man's actions are ambiguous. I've often walked away shaking my head from a conversation about sex or relationships with a straight man. I'd be completely confused about what he just said. At these times, my gay friends can really help clear things up, without being judgmental. Of course, they will not always tell me quite what I want to hear. I've had the experience of telling a gay friend something a man said to me, and having him just roll his eyes and say, 'Honey, get a grip. All guys say that.' But more often it's the reverse; I'll relate the story of some guy who rambled on endlessly to me about his day, and my friends will say, 'Honey, don't you realize, that's a guy-version of intimacy!' Whatever their advice, it is always delivered in a way that makes me laugh.

Gay men often like being able to play the "big brother" role. Adam, who has had occasion to coach his female friends, told us, "When my straight women friends ask me for advice about who to date, I feel useful, because I know how men think without feeling like I'm betraying my side or giving away any trade secrets — well, I am, but I'm not."

On the flip side, gay men can turn to their female friends and divulge their insecurities and weaknesses without the judgment they might receive from other men. Stuart, a self-proclaimed worry-wart, said to us, "My female friends know what it is like to sit by the phone, waiting for it to ring. They know that you are sometimes powerless in a relationship, and they don't think less of me for being in a vulnerable position with a particular man. Women can understand when I am nervous about my appearance or whether a guy finds me attractive. Many men, even my gay friends, don't think I should care about those things. They get really rational: 'If he's the right guy, he'll love you for you.' But my women friends understand that it's sometimes just illogical why you get hung up on a particular person who may or may not have any interest in you."

Straight women also have very strong opinions about their gay friend's boyfriends — sometimes positive, sometimes not. They bring their own standards and expectations to bear when judging their friend's boyfriends, even when they don't necessarily apply. Even Laura admits to being a bit over-protective of her buddy Shawn: "When I first met my friend Shawn's boyfriend, I didn't like him very much. He spent the entire dinner party talking about how attractive he found this new young man he was working with and how he'd like to seduce him. I got really offended: why was he talking about this other guy in front of, and instead of, my friend? As a woman, this would be a really unforgivable sin. Can you imagine if your girlfriend's boyfriend went on all evening about how much he'd like to seduce his new female secretary? But my gay friends told me that it was totally acceptable to talk about other men. In fact, it was sort of a ritual they all went through together. Talking about it definitely didn't mean they were acting on it, which I don't think is necessarily a good assumption with straight men. I've since gotten to know this guy and I adore him. I've also learned he's a big talker, but he really loves my friend the most."

Margaret told us of her best friend's boyfriend, who got a definite "thumbs down" from her. She said, "Bob had his first real experience with a man, and it was a guy who seemed to have something really wrong with him. He was really weird and had all these secrets, like a scar from an accident he wouldn't talk about. I was convinced he was doing drugs. Then Bob brought him to my house, and I tried to be nice, but rather than socialize, this guy slept all weekend. We'd get on the subway, he'd fall asleep, he'd go anywhere and be bored. I'd be looking at this guy and thinking, 'I'm not going to say anything, because it's Bob's first boyfriend.' I also had to ask myself, 'Am I jealous because he's spending time with another person? Am I afraid that the other person will get something I have.' I really had to step back and say to myself, 'OK, don't say anything, let him deal with this until he's ready to ask.'

"Finally one night, Bob and I were alone while this guy slept. Bob turned to me and said, 'I think you and I have spoiled each other for other human beings. Because after the way you treat me, and what we give to each other, I expect that with other people, and I'm not getting it.' His relationship with this guy ended shortly thereafter."

No one likes it when doubts about a friend's boyfriend prove correct. Yet most straight women and gay men have "been there and done that" in their own romantic lives, and know just what to say to a friend in each situation. And if that situation calls for them to be, shall we say, a bit "bitchy," so be it, and boyfriend beware!

Dishing the Dirt and Other Pastimes

Gay men and straight women are usually very honest with one another about their friend's boyfriends, although they may wisely wait until they are asked to give their opinion. But one of the best things about these friendships is that gay men and straight women can really dish the dirt about men in general when it's called for. And while gay men, as we will explain later, are sometimes guarded in sharing the most intimate and specific details of gay sex with their female friends, rarely is either partner sheepish about sharing the, shall we say,

"Being able to talk with a man about my sexual disasters or disappointments really helps somehow. He can put it into perspective"

shortcomings of the men in their lives. Candace echoed the sentiments of many friends we interviewed (and no doubt confirmed many a straight guy's worst fears) when she said, "We can talk about who is good in bed, who is bad in bed, who has a small penis or doesn't know what to do with it — all without feeling it reflects badly on us." Pamela likewise told us, "Being able to talk with a man about my sexual disasters or disappointments really helps somehow. He can put it into perspective, laugh about it, and make me feel like all men aren't going to hate me because it happened, because he doesn't hate me for it."

This sort of talk is in contrast to friendships between girlfriends, which can sometimes be more guarded. Josie admitted to us, "There is a feeling of disloyalty to the man in your life to dish about him sexually to another woman. I simply don't feel that when I'm talking to a gay man. Maybe on some level it's because the gay man is an outsider to the situation. He's never going to sleep with this guy, whereas all women, including my girlfriends, are potential sexual partners of his. There is also a level of embarrassment when admitting to a girlfriend that the men who find you attractive are inadequate sexually."

Gay men often accept a woman's desire for a purely physical relationship with a man more readily than will some of her girlfriends, who often think that she really wants, or should want, a more permanent commitment. One very honest (but anonymous) woman told us, "My female friends, particularly the married ones with children, don't understand that I like being single and childless. With my gay friends, there is none of that pressure, or worse, that pity. I can tell them of my various sexual encounters with men without knowing the response is going to be, 'OK, but when are you going to settle down?'"

On this issue, Rob was even more blunt concerning his friend Marcy from college. "Oh I was definitely against my friend Marcy settling down. Some of it was selfish, of course. I didn't want to lose my partner-in-crime, but also she had come from such a restrictive upbringing, and now in the big city, hanging out with me and my friends, she was having so much fun. There was a definite wild woman in there and I just didn't want to see it extinguished by some boring old boyfriend or relationship thing. In fact, it became kind of a joke, because I'd be encouraging her to play the field and she'd tease me by saying, 'No more fabulous meaningless sex. Don't make me have any more meaningless sex, please. Not again!' Maybe because I'm a man, maybe because I'm a gay man, but I sort of felt that it was my duty to help her live all of herself out fully. I really just don't know if any of her girlfriends, and certainly any kind of straight boyfriend, would have really done that. And the fact is, in my opinion, it was the best thing that could have ever happened to her, because when she finally met Don, the guy she ended up marrying, she knew the field. She wasn't going in with her eyes closed. She knew what was up, top to bottom, so to speak. And I'll take some credit for that."

Having moved out of conventional roles and expectations themselves, gay men can definitely be a great source of support, encouragement and advice for a woman when she wants to redefine the boundaries of what she "should" and "shouldn't" do. A sheer, unabashed enjoyment of sensuality and adventure, coupled with a refusal to be judgmental, can make gay men truly a woman's best friend in this arena. And women can offer their gay friends informed advice about the rituals and rewards of dating men. After all, straight women have been resolving romantic entanglements with the male of the species since they started playing doctor in the third grade, making them invaluable sources of dating "do's and don'ts" for their gay friends.

Meet Mr. Right

When a woman is ready for a serious relationship, who better than her gay male friends to help that happen? Who knows better what kind of man will be attracted to her and whom she will find attractive? And let's face it, who would have better taste in the men who should be introduced to her as a prospective mate than her gay friends? Laura has lots of stories about being fixed up by her gay friends. "When my gay friends want to introduce me to a man, I know he's gonna be straight, and I know he's gonna be cute. They fix me up with someone *they'd* want to be with if he were gay. However, there is sometimes some skepticism when a gay man wants to introduce you to a man who is a close friend of his, because you

"If you could find a man who genuinely loves your gay friend for the same reasons you do, but who would prefer to sleep with you, that would be perfect!"

know so few straight men who are interested in having gay friends: why does this guy? But if you could find a man who genuinely loves your gay friend for the same reasons you do, but who would prefer to sleep with you, that would be perfect!"

Cathie's gay best friend Matt introduced her to the man who eventually became her husband. Then he not-so-gently nudged her into a relationship. Cathie laughed, "He forced my husband on me. He kept saying I hope you get married!" In his own defense, Matt responded, "But he adored you in the way that you should be adored and loved you in the way you should be loved. I just saw that from the beginning."

Less frequent, from what we hear, but no less important, are the occasions when women introduce gay friends to one another. Stuart told us, "I think it is hilarious when my female friend tries to fix me up with men – particularly since she seems to concentrate solely on looks, ignoring the little details like age, intelligence, and employment prospects. But she certainly does know a cute guy when she sees one."

Women love to play matchmaker but are sometimes careful when it comes to their gay friends. Laura reluctantly confessed the following, "I'm always a bit hesitant to introduce my gay friends to one another. Many of my gay friends are either in theatre, and may already know each other, or else they are lawyers and businessmen. So any man I would introduce to them would come from outside their world and might have less in common with them. Plus there is always an uncomfortable aspect because gay men are the minority. I don't want my gay friends to think I'm just assuming all gay men are compatible with one another. I have introduced larger groups of gay men from different parts of my life to each other, letting my theatre friends meet my other friends at a party, and this has worked better than a one-on-one fix-up – plus it is fascinating and surprising to see who hooks up with whom."

Josie, on the other hand, goes at matchmaking with abandon. She admits, "I introduce all my gay friends to one another whenever I can, suggesting we meet for a drink or whatever. There are too many crazy guys out there, straight and gay, and I want to make sure my friend gets one of the good ones."

However these fix-ups may work out, you can bet that the two friends will get together afterward to dish all the delicious details of the encounter. After all, flirtations, infatuations, and romantic relationships may come and go, but chances are that the friendship between a straight woman and a gay man will outlast them all.

5. Romancing Each Other

Ask any woman, and she'll tell you that she tries not to make too many direct comparisons between the gay and straight men in her life: after all, gay men are incomparable! But one comparison is inescapable: gay men are simply more attentive, demonstrative, and unabashedly romantic

Both straight women and gay men report exchanging the words "I love you" with their friends every time they see each other, yet the meaning remains surprisingly free of dilution.

with women than their straight counterparts. This attentiveness and romanticism was illustrated the other evening when Laura invited a gay friend to the theatre. "He thanked me most graciously for the evening and mentioned repeatedly what good company I was, how attractive I looked, and what a good time he was having. The next day, he called our mutual gay male friend to thank him for introducing us. This behavior is remarkable, and yet typical; from a gay man I had dinner with recently, I received a postcard upon which he had written, 'It is always such a pleasure to spend an evening with a beautiful woman.'

"This stands in marked contrast to a discussion I'd had a few days earlier with a straight male friend," Laura continues. "I had fixed him up on a blind date with one of my girlfriends. He called *me* to tell me that he thought she was beautiful, intelligent and charming, with the clear expectation that I would pass the comments along. I asked whether he planned to call her again, and he responded in a typical, straight male fashion, telling me, 'The morning after our date, I left her a message on her home machine when I knew she'd be at work, thanking her for the evening. I plan to call her in one week and ask her out for the next week. I can't call her sooner than a week, because she might think I'm too eager, or develop expectations that I'm going to call every day. But if I wait for more than a week, she might think I didn't like her. Don't you think?'"

Is it any wonder that straight women seek the companionship of gay men, who shower them with compliments, appreciation, and affection? To be fair, it should be noted that most straight women would be much less likely to compliment a straight man on anything too personal for fear he might misinterpret but will freely compliment a gay man on his clothes, looks, even his body, without hesitation. This relief from fear of embarrassment or rejection not only provides a great ego boost for both parties but also makes it far easier for gay men and straight women to openly share their loving feelings about each other.

Both straight women and gay men report exchanging the words "I love you" with their friends every time they see each other, yet the meaning remains surprisingly free of dilution. They mean it — they aren't just saying it. Some onlookers may doubt this is true and dismiss such affection as an insincere "kiss-kiss" kind of gay and female affectation. But there is more often than not genuine love in this relationship, proving that relationships do not have to be sexual to be very romantic, or even seductive, in nature.

Perhaps the character of George put it best in the film *My Best Friend's Wedding* when he gave his best female friend, Julianne, his description of their relationship: "Maybe there won't be marriage. Maybe there won't be sex. But by God, there'll be dancing!"

Getting Sentimental!

One quality gay men share with their women friends is thoughtfulness. Meredith described her relationship with her best friend, Mike, as a limitless series of small kindnesses and considerate gestures that clearly demonstrate his affection for, and understanding of, the woman she really is. For example, she once took a long vacation in Europe

Gay men send flowers, write letters, remember birthdays and pick up that little something special their female friend has been looking all over town for. Women do these same things for their gay friends.

and was gone for several months. When she returned, there was a letter from Mike waiting in which he had enclosed a recording of a favorite song of theirs that described his feelings: "Miss You Like Crazy."

Equally thoughtful, Meredith gave Mike a "memory jar," a glass jar filled with scraps of paper on which she had written brief memories they had shared over the years. Every time Mike opened one, he would call and leave her a message sharing his memories and echoing her sentiments about each event. These two friends keep in constant touch. Meredith says, "I talk to him every week. We have email, voicemail and his cell phone, so we are always communicating, and we write each other. He writes more letters than I do. I'm not as good at it, but he is good at it and is articulate in a way I could never be, because he is a really creative, talented person. He writes the most beautiful, sensitive letters, and they are always incredibly supportive of me and what I'm going through. And I leave messages, knowing that he will always call me right back in a second."

Gay men send flowers, write letters, remember birthdays and pick up that little something special their female friend has been looking all over town for. Women do these same things for their gay friends. While some of this behavior would be considered overly sentimental and sappy by some people, or even obsessive and intrusive between a straight couple, gay men and straight women don't appear to be afraid of this interpretation.

Emotional Bravery

Perhaps there is an emotional bravery about "out" gay men which permits them to say, "I am not afraid of admitting whom I love, whether this is a love for another man or for my female friends." But even gay men who are not "out" seem to bathe their women friends in this thoughtfulness. In these cases, their overt affection stems less

One striking aspect of the friendship between gay men and straight women is their ability to quickly "click" as friends and then go the extra mile to pursue the friendship.

from bravery and more from a genuine appreciation of this woman friend and of the "heterosexuality" of their valued and comfortable relationship. In both cases, "out" or not, gay men make a space for their female friends to express the full range of their emotions and to indulge their romantic inclinations with a receptive partner.

This emotional bravery, this deep appreciation of their women friends, enables gay men to use the "c" word — commitment — a word that makes many straight men break out in a cold sweat. In committing themselves to their friends — establishing regular dates, keeping up with special occasions like birthdays and holidays, demonstrating their presence in big and small ways over a long time — gay men provide their female friends with a level of emotional security that can be lacking in many straight man-woman relationships.

Women are frequently amazed at the ability of gay men to hold onto relationships, even with ex-lovers. Ellen describes her reaction to the relationship between her friend Frank and Gary, his "ex." "Frank remained good friends with Gary after they broke up. I was always amazed at how prevalent it was for gay men that former lovers stayed in touch or remained friends, even with their new lovers around. In the heterosexual world, once you broke up with somebody, that was it. With straight couples, it was very rare that people stayed in touch with each other without jealousy or other problems. But with my gay friends, there were such strong bonds between them, bonds that went beyond the sexual. I envied that, and I thought it was very special that Frank and Gary could remain so close to each other, because then, though the love relationship had ended, they didn't lose each other from their lives."

Gay men bring a similar level of commitment to their relationships with their women friends. Patrick, a gay man with a select group of female friends, describes his feelings toward them this way. "There is an absoluteness to my relationships, in the sense that I don't think that any of the women whom I love have even a moment's doubt about me loving them. I cannot stop loving somebody; I've never been able to stop. I don't start very easily, and I don't love very many people. I hear people say you're lucky if you have two good friends. Well I have ten or maybe even twenty. I have a few other people I'm civil with but not very many, and the rest of them are completely outside my world. They're not on the radar screen. But when I love someone, it's absolute and unconditional. My relationships with women are so personal, and none of them are alike. The only thing they have in common is that we deeply love each other. I feel completely accepted by my straight women friends."

Women involved in these relationships are similarly brave in their ability to share their emotions freely with a man. While it seems increasingly difficult for women to express their romantic natures without being the subject of ridicule as Harlequin-romance-reading lightweights, at the same time, they are supposed to covet the attention of, and be desirable to, men. Thus, many women these days find themselves torn in two directions. On the one hand, they are raised on the fairy tale notions of romantic love, to be on the lookout for their Prince Charming, and to use certain long-standing "rules" to snag him. On the other hand, they are supposed to be rational, smart women who don't make foolish choices and who maintain their identity separate and apart from men.

Given these conflicting expectations, it often takes a real leap of faith for a woman to openly and honestly express her affection for any man, including the gay men in her life. One striking aspect of the friendship between gay men and straight women is, therefore, their ability to quickly "click" as friends and then go the extra mile to pursue the friendship. As the stories we've heard illustrate, once these friends have connected with each other in this inexpressible way, this connection often ripens into a full-fledged friendship, because the woman is brave enough to go out on a limb with a gay man to let him know her interest in having a friendship. Such an expression of interest can be quite an act of courage on the part of a woman, who has probably been taught to be reluctant to call men at all, much less to call one and say she would like to see more of him. With gay men, though, a woman is free to overcome her wariness about being forward with her feelings.

Laura tells this story of her own experience. "I first met my friend Chad, who is gay, at a Christmas party, and we started chatting. Before we knew it, we had 'clicked' in that special way you do when you meet someone you know is likely to be in your life for some time. We immediately "got" each other's humor and spoke in the same rhythms. We had the same artistic taste in theatre. More important, we hated the same people. At the end of the evening, we exchanged numbers and agreed to keep in touch. I called him the next day to make sure he knew that I meant it, and that I really did want to pursue the friendship. I would rarely do this with a straight man, and certainly never with one I was romantically interested in. This is more than just societal conditioning; it's what experience has taught me is the way to proceed to which men are most receptive. My experience with my gay friends is really helping me to become more open and brave about expressing my desire to see any of my friends, including the straight men in my life."

Yet for all their honesty, bravery and ability to communicate, it seems that gay men and straight women are suddenly tongue-tied and secretive when one certain subject comes up, which poses the question: Are the secrets we keep more telling than the truths we share?

6. Keeping Secrets From One Another

How can two friends be so close and share so much with one another, yet keep certain important parts of their lives so separate and secret?

Since "just getting together to talk" is one of the major activities gay men and straight women do a lot together, it is intriguing that we found certain secret things gay men and straight women *don't* tend to talk to each other about. On the face of it, you would think some of these subjects would merit a great deal of discussion, but time and again we noticed their absence. How can two friends be so close and share so much with one another, yet keep certain important parts of their lives so separate and secret?

The Forbidden Topic

One of the most significant "forbidden" topics we discovered was the intimate and graphic details of the sex lives of gay men. Love lives? No problem. These are discussed endlessly. Sex lives? Well, many gay men share the who's, what's, and where's of their romantic conquests with their female friends, but there seems to be a line somewhere that is rarely crossed, a line that is difficult to define with precision. For one thing, it seems clear that gay "sex toys" and/or sexual practices which exclusively pertain to gay rather than heterosexual sex are far less frequently discussed.

Gay men don't tend to talk about the nitty-gritty of their sex lives with their women friends, and the question naturally arises: why?

Rob, for example, was stunned to learn that Laura was not familiar with a particular gay sex toy mostly certainly used by many gay men, presumably including at least some of Laura's gay friends. Laura responded, "I've heard so many details of my gay friends' sex lives, including who they've slept with, how many times, and all that, but when one of them tries to tell me about things that are kind of graphic, the other guys shush him up. In fact, after Rob explained the ins and outs of this particular toy, I called one of my closest gay friends and complained, 'Hey, why are you keeping me in ignorance?' And he replied, 'Oh, I thought you knew about them.' This prompted his significant other, also my close friend, who was listening to our conversation — you can never talk to one of them without the other one putting his two cents in — to yell at his boyfriend, 'Oh how crude! Don't say those things to her!' The same thing happened when a group of us, including these guys, were out to dinner and one of them started telling me a hilarious story about a hotel room, a conspicuously visible sex toy and the hotel's maid service. No sooner had he launched into the story than half the guys at the table started shushing him, and the others started squirming or giggling. The storyteller was quickly silenced."

Laura continues: "I recently tried to help my most overprotective gay friend to 'get over it,' by taking him up on his long-time offer for the two of us to visit a notorious gay strip club. We sat together watching these dancers, and I noticed he was chatting nervously about their costumes, their moves, and occasionally about their, shall we say, physical attributes. He really tried to be brave and comfortable about my being there. Yet no sooner did one of the dancers bend over in an effort to display a particularly intimate part of his anatomy, that my friend screamed out: 'Laura, don't look!' and forcefully clamped his hands over my eyes. I have to admit, I find his protective nature very loving and endearing, even if it does mean I miss the occasional opportunity to expand my knowledge of male exotic dancers."

Laura's experience with overprotective gay friends turned out to be typical. Most of the women we talked to rarely heard the most intimate and gay-specific details of their gay male friends' sexual encounters. Gay men don't tend to talk about the nitty-gritty of their sex lives with their women friends, and the question naturally arises: why? One would hardly think that gay men would as a group so purposefully avoid such a subject, especially with their women friends since, as we have just seen, they feel the freedom to talk with these women easily and comfortably about almost anything else.

This idea that many gay men avoid talking in too much detail about sex with women is interesting in itself. It is an even more striking omission when one takes into account how a certain kind of hypersexuality is often a point of personal pride for contemporary gay men and, in an even wider way, how being sexual is practically a political strategy on the part of the gay male community. Rob's own experience illustrates this. "When we talk among ourselves, sex is rarely far away from the center of the discussion. Even at the most elegant, formal gay male dinner parties, it is not at all unheard of to be swapping proctologist stories or playing 'can-you-top-this?': 'You did it in an elevator? Well, I did it in a taxicab.' 'Taxicab? Ha! I did it with my ex in the hallway before a job interview!' If you go out with another gay male friend, either or both of you are being constantly distracted by hunks walking past the table, sitting in front of you, driving past; indeed, it is practically de rigueur to fantasize aloud about what, how and how many times. If you talk about a male friend to someone, inevitably there comes the question, 'So is he cute?' A conversation with a gay male friend without a 'woof' at someone means something is severely wrong — one of you is depressed and desperately in need of help. Even in gay professional circles, at high level meetings or conferences I have attended, there is a tacit expectation that a level of sexual awareness and humor is not only welcome but required."

Much of this, of course, is due to the fact that among out gay men, maintaining a very sex-positive attitude in the face of a very sex-negative culture is an essential part of self-acceptance. Rob explains. "We spent many years not expressing ourselves, our desires, our interests and our responses. In coming out, most of us make damn sure that we aren't going back to those times ever again. If the effect is sometimes rather tiresome and adolescent in the eyes of others — others, by the way, who had the luxury of a normal adolescence — most of us don't really care. We feel entitled to recapture the 'oohs,' 'aahs,' and 'isn't he hot' in our adulthood. True, I am often called upon as a therapist to try to guide certain gay men into a bit more of a mature sexuality, but the ability to be sexual and to talk about sex — in sometimes obsessive, microscopic, gasp-producing detail — is an enduring joy that most gay men these days could never be convinced to forgo."

Rob continues: "If what we missed in adolescence means the way that our sex lives frequently occupy a place at the forefront of our personal con- sciousness, on the level of the gay community, the emphasis on sexuality and sexual freedom repre- sents nothing less than a political and social agenda for gay men. It was clear twenty-five years ago at the start of the Gay Liberation movement and it is even more clear nowadays: our difference from the major- ity of people around us boils down to something essentially sexual. Of course, there is no arguing that this sexual difference has very complex and far- reaching implications which go far beyond the bed- room and touch upon nearly all areas of our lives. And yet, cultivating a large and fertile place for sex in our lives and relationships has been at the heart of nearly all our political activism."

One might debate whether or not gay men using sexuality as a political strategy are wise or foolish, effective or self-defeating, or even true; for many gay men, sex is *not* at the forefront of their hearts, minds and lives. It occupies rather an important, but by no means central, place in their personality and relationships. However, whether or not you agree with this marriage of sex and identity, the fact remains that sex is front and center in contemporary male gay culture, front and center in our political and cultural efforts, and, for many of us, front and center in our personal lives. Except, it seems, when gay men sit down with their straight women friends.

We found it a bit startling that gay men, of *all* people, would suddenly start editing themselves, holding back, leaving certain things to the imaginations of their female friends. One explanation may be found in the fact that, after all, gay men are just that — men. They too experience the social pressure to act like "gentlemen" around women, and clearly understanding what is appropriate locker-room conversation with the guys versus what is appropriate talk when women are around. With their women friends, gay men may refrain from the explicit discussion of sexual matters they indulge in with their peers more out of politeness than anything else. They may well sense that most of their female friends do not want all of the details of gay sex, any more than women would expect their gay friend to be interested in their menstrual cycles and associated activities. In online terms, it's all ALBTMI — A Little Bit Too Much Information. Thus, rather than specifically avoiding or suppressing themselves in the presence of their women friends, gay men do what women would sometimes like straight men to do more often in their presence: they pick up on women's feelings and respect them.

For every rule, however, there are myriad exceptions. That is true about this generalization as well. When Rob asked his friend Harriet whether or not her gay friends dared to talk to her about sex, she responded unequivocally, "They very definitely talk to me about sex. Some consider me like a sister, some like a mother, and, for some, I am like the wife or the girlfriend that they didn't have. Because they can talk to me about just about everything and anything, some of my gay friends have said to me, 'I wish I could find a man like you.' I laugh, 'Well, that's gonna be a problem.' Because I am not a man and there are some differences in how we have been conditioned to be in the world, our ways of being supportive, nurturing and close with each other can feel very different sometimes."

Some gay men feel quite uninhibited with their female friends, going so far as to share graphic details about sex or even acting as "sex coaches" for their grateful female friends. After all, as the character of Elaine complained on the television series *Seinfeld*, men have more frequent access to "the equipment" than women do; why shouldn't they give women helpful hints on how that equipment operates? Another great example can be found in the highly entertaining (and educational) book, *Sex Tips for Straight Women from a Gay Man* by Dan Anderson and Maggie Berman. They write, "The only truly accurate way to learn the sexual tricks of the trade, or what makes a guy really moan, is to go straight to the source: a man. This man needs to be someone special, who not only knows his own preferences but who has had the opportunity to know the preferences of a number of other guys. Who better than an honest-to-goodness gay man? He knows things most straight guys don't even know about themselves."[4]

And as one grateful (and, we're guessing, popular) woman we interviewed noted, "Everything I ever learned about blow jobs I learned from my gay friends. I do ask gay men about gay sex – 'what's good for you?' Because I figure, he's still a man and he likes basically the same sorts of stimulation. So if you're interested in it you would go to the pro. So I ask and they always tell me, and I've tried it and it works!"

Clearly some gay men and straight women are quite frank in their discussions about sex. Yet from what we discovered in most of our conversations, such free-wheeling sex talks are very much the exception rather than the rule.

Unveiling the Mystery

For many such friends, the discussion of sex is off-limits entirely. Various women and men give reasons like, "Well, he's a very private person," or "It's just not the sort of thing I discuss with anyone." In other words, it is

Are they choosing to act like good boys to gain Mommy's approval? Or are they truly honoring and respecting their friends' feelings?

not just that the down-and-dirty details of the deed are withheld, but some friends do not discuss sexuality at all: their relationships with husbands and boyfriends, and their romantic problems, yes; but sex in all its juicy splendor, no.

For Rob, there is some concern about the general pattern of sex being off-limits as a topic for woman and gay men. "One of the consequences of this, I fear, is that our straight women friends often have no idea of the vast preoccupation gay men have with sex. After a while, they may begin to start thinking of their gay male friends as 'good little boys' or worse, as their personal 'pet eunuchs' — perfect creatures who have all the best attributes of men without any of those nasty 'other' aspects."

Pre-Gay Lib depictions of the friendship between gay men and women certainly had a great deal of this particular flavor. In E. F. Benson's various Lucia novels, Lucia's closest friend was the very gay but very closeted Georgie — an English provincial dandy who specialized in needlepoint, retired each Saturday night to dye his hair and loved nothing more than to gossip with Lucia about the comings-and-goings of their fellow inhabitants of Riseholme. But what Lucia herself refers to as "that horrid little thing which Freud calls sex" is never openly discussed.[5] Many couples in these old movies had their one gay friend, the sissy who gets mistaken for a lothario, the prissy butler who always saved the day, the obviously gay sidekick who is pursued by the amorous spinster, but to even suggest that these characters had sex lives would be unthinkable. Obviously gay characters were desexed in order to make them palatable or amusing, a maneuver that is highly problematic when applied to real gay men in everyday life.

So one has to wonder if it is gay men who are removing the most intimate details of sex from the discussion with their female friends or whether it is the women who are choosing to ignore or overlook a significant part of their gay male friends' actual lives. Is it simply that gay men don't bring that part of themselves to the cafe or the theater when they meet with their women friends, saving it instead for other times and other places? Are they choosing to act like good boys to gain Mommy's approval? Or are they truly honoring and respecting their friends' feelings?

From the other side of the equation, though, we have to wonder whether women in fact resist having these discussions out of discomfort. Some women we interviewed who are very comfortable talking with their gay friends about sex are less comfortable watching public displays of affection between men, which they still find strange and new. It may be, of course, that women refrain from seeking out the details of gay sex out of respect and politeness. Women may not want to invade their friends' privacy or have them think they find their gay male friends a curiosity or aberration to be deposed and examined. Women want their gay friends to know that they accept their lifestyle unconditionally, so there could be a reticence to ask too many questions for fear that their friend will misinterpret her as having doubts, judging, or even preparing to reject him. Women may well be avoiding the subject out of fear, of not understanding, of saying the wrong thing, or of asking the wrong question.

Laura notes that women in general seem less anxious to define themselves in relation to sexuality than many gay men do, perhaps because society is so often trying to impose this definition on women without their consent. Unlike those portions of the gay community who celebrate their sexuality as a political statement, there is no "Pro-Bimbo" political movement for women. If anything, much feminist thinking runs in quite the opposite direction. Whereas gay men are willing to put the focus on their sexuality, women have to constantly struggle against attempts to objectify them as sexual beings, whether by men, other women, or by the media, fashion magazines, movies and television. Women themselves are particularly dismissive toward another woman who defines herself in an overtly sexual way. So sexuality would not necessarily be the first thing a woman is going to focus on when dealing with any person, whether it's another woman or a gay man.

Most women also have been trained from an early age that they must preserve their "mystery" and that the most alluring woman is one who holds certain things back. As noted above, these "mysteries" have always included the most intimate details of her reproductive cycles, referred to obliquely as "female troubles" or "women's things." Regarding these, many women have felt some shame and embarrassment around men, using such quaint euphemisms as "my aunt from Red Bank is visiting," "it's time for my friend," or "my monthly visitor is in town." The mere fact that a man happens to be gay does not necessarily make some women feel any more comfortable discussing such intimate mysteries with him. So, if some women hold back from the most explicit sexual discussions, it may be because of the most obvious reason: this friend is, after all, a card-carrying member of the opposite sex.

7. Flirting With Each Other

 Given that this friend- ship involves a man and a woman, the question invariably arises: "So how platonic *is* this friendship,

Another equally powerful factor often comes into play: mutual physical attraction

anyway?" The answer to that question reveals one of the most charming idiosyncrasies in the friendships between gay men and straight women. For no sooner does one of these friends state, "Oh, no, there is no sexual tension in the relationship" or "Our friendship is delightfully free of that male-female nonsense," that they'll admit how keenly aware they are that their friend is an attractive member of the opposite sex. And while most of these friends choose each other primarily for the same reasons anyone would choose a friend, including compatibility and similar interests, it is evident that another equally powerful factor often comes into play: mutual physical attraction.

The Attraction Factor

People naturally gravitate toward people they find physically attractive, whether we're talking about choosing someone to date, choosing someone as a friend, or even interviewing someone for a job. We would have a hard time denying that "looks-ism" is prevalent in our society, and women and gay men,

> *Men and women, when choosing partners, not only choose people they find attractive but also choose people whom they believe others will find attractive.*

with their highly attuned aesthetic senses, frequently admit that how the other one looked was a key component in their initially coming together as friends. Can it be a coincidence that all their friends just happen to be someone they think is gorgeous?

Men and women, when choosing partners, not only choose people they find attractive but also choose people whom they believe *others* will find attractive. It's the high school thing — wanting to date the cutest boy or girl in the school as a way of establishing that you yourself are attractive or otherwise worthy. After all, if this great-looking person is walking down the street with you, you must have something on the ball. This phenomenon is evident in the friendships between straight women and gay men, who frequently describe their friend's beauty or attractiveness when telling the tale of their first meeting — something two girlfriends or male buddies rarely do.

One of the first things Ann told us about why she and her friend Brad became friends after initially meeting at the arts reception was, "Besides his readily apparent intelligence and insightfulness, I liked the way he looked. He was scrubbed, clean, and well-groomed, and had a good physique. He was obviously a man who took care of himself, and I like that in my friends."

From her own experience, Laura tells this story. "I first met one of my good friends when he was in New York starring in a play about a group of gay men. I thought he was good-looking on stage, but many people are. As another actor friend says,

"Good lighting, great makeup and good old-fashioned distance can hide a lot." So I was surprised when I walked into the lobby bar of the Algonquin Hotel and saw this man, and several of his friends, sitting there. They were all, in a word, gorgeous – lounging together on a sofa, drinking, smiling and laughing. I was thinking about getting involved in producing the play in California, and having just seen the play that evening, I introduced myself to him. He and his friends were unbelievably charming, and although I knew from the outset that they were gay, I think the fact that they were so attractive played a role in my willingness to go over and say hello – to go the extra mile to meet them. I'm a bit less reluctant to approach men I think are attractive. Of course, it is easier when you think the men are gay, because you feel confident that they won't assume you are coming on to them. Plus, many gay men really like women, so you just know a warm welcome is awaiting you."

For straight women, one of the perks of spending time with gay men is that they often find themselves surrounded by good-looking, well-dressed and charming men who seek out and enjoy the company of women. Laura continues the story of her own group of friends. "The element of physical attraction plays an undeniable role in my relationships with gay men. I find it energizing to be around attractive men of all descriptions, whether they are gay or straight, married or available. Many of my gay friends are actors, dancers, and other performers, and they are often incredibly handsome with great bodies and impeccable taste in clothes. One evening a few years ago, I went to see my friend, the one I'd met at the Algonquin and who had since become a close friend, who was then starring on Broadway in a hit musical. After the show, he and I and about a dozen of his actor friends went out to dinner to celebrate. We were seated at a big round table in the middle of a bustling restaurant in the heart of the theatre district. I recall suddenly being struck by the fact that I was surrounded by a dozen of the best looking men in New York, or anywhere. Everyone in the restaurant was staring at us (and thinking, I'll bet, "you lucky girl"), which is not unusual when I'm with this group of friends. All of these guys give off this incredible male energy and are wonderfully charismatic. When one of my friends and I walk down Fifth Avenue in New York, people literally turn their heads to stare at him. I've had the same experience with a friend in San Francisco. The fact that these men are so attractive gives them a level of confidence and self-assurance that I find compelling and even contagious. I feel more attractive, and have more self-confidence, in their company."

In high school, Cathie was friends with a gay man, who is now her best friend. Just as she does now, she clearly found him attractive then. She said, "I never knew he was gay when I knew him in high school. He always had the pretty girlfriends, he was the star in the school play, and he had this rock band. The girls were just so crazy for him."

Of course, being around anyone *that* gorgeous can try the patience of a saint. As Margaret told us, "It can drive you nuts, because I look at them and wonder — how much do you aerobicize? How did you get that way? They do have better thighs, and sometimes they don't deserve the perfect thighs they have."

Yet women are willing to tolerate the genetically thin-thighed, because they are so darned good looking. As Candace put it, "Most of my gay friends are extraordinarily attractive. I just gravitate toward men I find attractive, straight or gay, married or single. I enjoy the male attention from my gay friends, and this is enhanced when they are attractive. I don't find myself attracted to them; I'm just always aware of how good looking they are, and somehow this makes me feel more attractive myself."

Similarly, gay men often make friends with women they find attractive or beautiful. Contrary to the stereotype which holds that gay men are gay because they reject or hate women, many gay men have a real appreciation for beautiful women, whether she's a movie star or his close friend. Gay men love women on many levels, and their simple, unabashed physical appreciation of their female friends is notable. As Patrick says, "I am aesthetically attracted to all my straight women friends; I think they're beautiful. My friends tend to be beautiful, but I don't know what that has to do with. My mother was beautiful — she looked like Greta Garbo — and she was one of five sisters who were known to be the most beautiful women in the area."

Gay men seem to have a particular affinity for women with classic "movie star" looks, and many gay men develop a real devotion to famous women who have an almost surreal or iconic beauty, although they might not necessarily gravitate to women who are sexually threatening. Gay men may connect to Madonna more than to Marilyn Monroe, prefer Judy Garland to Sophia Loren, or find Cher more to their taste than Pamela Anderson Lee. This may be due to the innocent, almost childlike, quality of the admiration of many gay men for these women.

Several of Laura's friends told her that they identified with women they considered beautiful and glamorous when they were children. More than merely appreciating beautiful movie stars, when these men were younger, they actually wanted to *be* Liza or Liz or Bette. And in sharing this insight from her friends with Rob over dinner, Rob laughed and said, "I know exactly what they are talking about. After all, I think that is definitely why drag has such a big place in the gay community. It's a complex issue, of course, but certainly one piece of it is definitely gay men's desire to be that glamorous, that *fabulous*, at least for a little while, and to get that sort of attention from men. Remember, the word 'fabulous' comes from the word 'fable' and I think there is a definite wish on the part of gay men in childhood to live out those Hollywood fairy tales of glamour, love and romance by *becoming* those stars."

Is it any wonder, then, that gay men later become friends with women they find beautiful? And gay men do more than just seek out and appreciate a beautiful woman; they reward her for that beauty with attention, compliments and affection. Lowell, a performance artist and filmmaker, was upfront about the appearance issue with his female friends. He said, "I love being with a striking-looking woman, walking into a restaurant or an industry event and turning heads, and frankly, I cultivate relationships with women who have a very in-your-face personal style. Not necessarily classic beauties but women who make a statement with how they look. These friends see their appearance as an assertion of who they are. That actually intimidates a lot of straight guys, because some of these women can really be sort of 'out there' at times with the hair and fashions. But I'm not intimidated nor are the rest of my gay friends. We love it, and these women know we do. At times, it's even a little bit like a contest — who can we shock the most and how? Very fun. Very fun."

So, in addition to being drawn toward their friends' inner beauty, gay men and straight women revel in their friends' outward physical beauty as well. Though one might not expect it from these friendships, this element of mutual physical appreciation is one of the livelier and most exciting parts of the connection between straight women and gay men.

The Generosity Quotient

Women love the attention they receive from their gay friends. Why not? These are not only men, but men with great taste! As Marcy told us, "Gay men appreciate what you've done with your hair, and it's nice to get male attention, whether it's straight or gay. It's always nice to be noticed by a man. It's not the same as two girlfriends because he's a man and I'm a woman and he gives me the man's point of view, even if it's the gay man's point of view. A lot of times it's not so different from the straight man's point of view. He may have more vocabulary to tell me about fashion designers and why he likes the dress and why the

These compliments from gay men are evidence of a deeper affection, signs that their gay friends appreciate her beauty inside and out.

hair's not working, where a straight man will say: 'I don't know.' It's all in the phraseology." In other words, as Laura puts it: "It's a treat for a woman, who has saved a month's salary to buy the Prada bag, to be out with a man who will say: 'Wow, what a gorgeous Prada bag. I swear it makes your hips look smaller!'"

This level of attention and appreciation is one of the major perks of these great friendships. As Laura describes it, "One of the greatest gifts my gay friends give is that they are amazingly vocal in their admiration for a woman they find beautiful. I don't think I've ever spent more than a half hour with any one of my close gay friends without them coming up with some compliment on my appearance — and believe me, at times this takes real effort. 'Great shoes' seems to be the all-purpose, fallback compliment when nothing else is working. Where straight men often dole out physical compliments as sparingly as if they were proposals of marriage, I find that gay men are exceedingly generous in their compliments and attentions toward their female friends."

On a number of different levels, women adore it when their gay friends think they look beautiful.

They love the attention from any man, gay or straight. They may find it important to be aesthetically pleasing to their gay friend, since for them, it's part of their role to always look as well dressed, coifed, and generally well turned out as their male friends do. But it seems that women can also accept these compliments more easily or comfortably from gay men. Gay men may be engaging in a bit of flattery, but deep down the woman knows he isn't after anything. He doesn't want something from her that she may be unwilling to give up. Plus, these compliments from gay men are evidence of a deeper affection, signs that her gay friends appreciate her beauty inside *and* out.

This was Margaret's experience with her gay friends. She told us, " They think you are beautiful because of the person you are inside. I mean they just love you for the person you are. It doesn't matter that you don't have thin thighs or whatever. I know a lot of gay men, and they're all obsessed with breasts for some reason. Like my friend, Bob. I think my breasts are in the way, they drive me nuts, and so when I lost weight and they shrunk, I was so happy – but he wasn't. We went to see the play *How I Learned to Drive* about a woman whose uncle had molested her, and she's talking about her boobs — and Bob was laughing, hysterically, because he could finally get it — OK, it's not just you, it drives other women crazy too. He had thought I was nuts for talking about it. Because gay men don't understand that when straight men talk at you, they are sometimes looking at your breasts. But gay men, they look you up and down, head to toe, and they're like: she's fine just the way she is. So I am very lucky to have spent so much time in that circle because it helped my self-esteem. If these guys think I'm OK, then I must be. Why can't straight men make me feel this good about myself?" When a gay man says to his friend, "You are so beautiful," she knows that he is talking about more than her dress. He's talking about her as a person, and it's the whole package he's finding beautiful.

In short, there comes a time when a woman needs to hear from a man that she is beautiful, even when she's looking a bit ragged; that she is desirable, even though she hasn't had a date in months; that she is intelligent, even when she has done something incredibly stupid. A woman may have to tell her gay friend what she needs to hear, or he may just know it without having to be told. This willingness to give her a "man's opinion," a positive, loving, supportive opinion, can really get her through the tough times.

Honey, Drape!

Yet, as nonjudgmental as gay men can be of women's appearance in some ways, they can also be highly critical in other ways. The same gay men who are able to consistently find something beautiful or admirable in any woman who takes care of herself can be a bit

Gay men are rarely dismissive or hostile, however much they may want to physically drag a woman into Bloomingdale's for a makeover.

harsh and unforgiving of women who really "let themselves go." Ironically, the very attitude of love and admiration for women and women's bodies may, by the same token, result in highly developed aesthetic sense that really wants everything to be a beautiful as possible. But even at their most judgmental, gay men don't seem to judge women in the dismissive and injurious way some straight men do.

Many a woman has had the experience of being dismissed as a nonentity because she is not young, thin or pretty in that "Baywatch" way many straight men covet. There is sometimes even a palpable hostility of straight men toward women they find unattractive (particularly prevalent in men who are themselves unattractive, may we point out). Gay men, on the contrary, are rarely as dismissive or hostile, however much they may want to physically drag a woman into Bloomingdale's for a makeover. They appear able to recognize the value of a woman as a person separate and apart from her physical appearance; a separation many straight men, who may be biologically-driven to evaluate all women to some degree as potential sex partners, find it difficult or impossible to manage.

Since a gay man really wants his female friend to be and feel beautiful, he may feel duty-bound to share his opinions on how she can achieve her fullest potential. Laura has many stories to tell about her "helpful" gay friends. "I was sitting there talking to a gay friend, and he suddenly started looking at the top of my head, instead of into my eyes, like there was a big bug sitting on my forehead. I stopped talking and asked, 'What the heck are you looking at?' and he said, 'How long has it been since you've had your highlights done?' On another day, I was shopping for evening gowns, and I found one I liked which was kind of a tube dress. I showed it to another gay friend and asked, 'Do you think my stomach will stick out?' And he took one look at my little tummy and said: 'Honey, drape.' Or in another incident that comes to mind: I used to work in an office with two gay men, and they were sweet, but they were always running in and saying, 'Oh we saw this great dress today you'd look great in,' which made me feel like I was their Barbie Doll and they wanted to play dress-up."

Women, of course, can be just as ruthless with their gay friends. As Jerry, a self-described gay, Jewish prince, told us, "I go out drinking with a friend, and suddenly she turns into my mother. 'Why are you wearing that same shirt? Why don't you buy some new clothes?' I may be gay, but it doesn't necessarily mean I like shopping any more than the next guy."

For other gay men and their straight women friends, shopping together, and helping the other to look their best, is one of their basic bonding rituals. When we asked Matt and Cathie what they did together, they responded, "Everything but get our legs waxed. And we do a lot of shopping together."

Many friends report shopping for wedding dresses and the killer black cocktail dress (both for her), interview suits and resort wear (except bathing suits — these friendships aren't quite *that* platonic!). They confer on hairstyles, accessories, tints and highlights, even plastic surgery.

Laura, for instance, relies heavily on her gay friends for support and advice on appearance issues. "My gay friends generally have a much more empowering relationship to physical appearance than that possessed by my straight male and female friends. There is much less of a "you're not a kid anymore, so it's over, and there's nothing you can do about it" attitude. Appearance is less an issue of destiny than of diligence, and they all work incredibly hard to maintain their physical appearance. For my friends who are performers, spending time at the gym and salon is more than a narcissistic pursuit; it is a job requirement. This makes them invaluable 'appearance coaches' for me, as they clearly believe any woman can be gorgeous if she devotes sufficient time and energy to the undertaking. Most importantly, they are willing to lie to me, and have an instinctive ability to know when to say 'Oh, my God, you're a stick' when I've just gained five pounds.

"On the other hand," Laura continues, "this empowering attitude means that they actually expect me to work out every day, and in public! A lot of my gay friends are really into the gym culture. It's not exercise, in the negative way I think of it, but more of a social club for them. So they can't understand why I don't want to go and work out at a public gym rather than skulking off to private sessions with my personal trainer. And I tell them, if I thought I was going to be surrounded by cute guys who want to 'spot' me so I can lift my barbells while simultaneously checking out my butt, I might feel differently about it."

A Very Rich Stew

Yet for all the focus on appearance, gay men and straight women seem able to achieve a delicate balance – maintaining awareness of physical beauty and mutual attraction while dispensing with sexual tension. Jack told us emphatically, "The great thing about these friendships is that there is no sexual tension. There is none. So you get to really know and be friends with another sex or another kind of person and understand them and love them without the complications of sex. It's more an emotional thing than an overtly sexual thing. It's an open emotional relationship with no strings. And it's nice to get attention from the opposite sex!"

There is absolutely no sexual tension — except when it's suddenly there. They are not attracted to each other — until they notice that they are.

Clearly whenever you get a woman and a man together, there are going to be some complications. Add to this the fact that not everybody is always straight or always gay all the time. Then factor in some alcohol, lowered inhibitions, and a strong curiosity factor, and you can have some really interesting encounters between two friends that go beyond mere flirtations. Josie, with characteristic candor, told us, "I have this one friend who is definitely gay and who has been in a long-term relationship with a man. But he clearly lusts after certain parts of my anatomy. Every once in a while, especially when he's had a couple of drinks, I'll catch him staring admiringly at my breasts or even patting me a little too slowly on the bottom. But he doesn't do it in a way I find offensive. He doesn't want to have sex with me. And he's not objectifying me. He just finds me a bit sexually attractive for a few moments. And this is flattering on the deepest level, because it reminds me that although we are friends, I am no less of a woman to him."

Gay men tell of getting drunk, making out with their female friends, and living to tell the tale — or not telling the tale, as none of the gay men we interviewed wished to be quoted as admitting this particular indiscretion. And for a supposedly platonic relationship, women ask gay men to do some pretty "un-platonic" things, like provide them with offspring. Patrick told us forthrightly, "One of my female friends wants to have kids, and she wants me to be a sperm donor. Several women have asked me to do this, and I don't have any problem with that; I think it shows they have wonderfully good taste. They say the gay gene is passed on the female side so maybe I wouldn't be able to propagate gay people. But if I could sire a gay son or daughter I would, because I think the world needs more gay people."

Some gay men have asked their women friends to marry them, for reasons of inheritance, citizenship, to improve their employment prospects, or to comply with religious or social pressure. Then there are some gay men and straight women who marry each other for a variety of reasons but maintain an agreement that they can go elsewhere for sex. Whether this is a true "friendship" is debatable.

What all these complications point out, however, is that the friendship between gay men and straight women is sometimes a very rich stew. There is absolutely no sexual tension — except when it's suddenly there. They are not attracted to each other — until they notice that they are. And they never judge one another about their looks — except when they do. But underneath it all there is a constancy that is missing in many other relationships with the opposite sex, even so-called platonic ones. For although gay men and their female friends may occasionally blur the lines a bit between platonic and otherwise, these friends understand that their romantic and sexual destinies lie along different paths, and acceptance of that fact ultimately enables their friendship to endure.

Yet the occasionally seductive relationship between gay men and their straight women friends can lead some women to be attracted to their gay friends in a way with which even they are not comfortable. And although most women never fall in love with their gay friends, there may be an unspoken attraction to them, or at the very least an unexpressed longing to find a straight man who is as easy to love as they are.

8. Testing the Limits of Love

We made sure to ask two questions of the women we inter- viewed: "Have you ever fallen in love with your gay male friends?" and "Have you talked about it with him?" We received a wide variety of responses.

What woman wouldn't be tempted by a wonderful, handsome, well- dressed, sensitive, talented, bright, and attentive gay male friend?

On one end of this spectrum were women like Ann who told us, "I have never had any romantic feelings for any of my gay friends. In fact, I've always thought it was sort of a joke. It also makes it easy to open up and become friendly without any of the sexual tension. Many of my friends look at some gay men and say: 'He's so cute" and many women want to change a gay man's mind. You know, the thinking that goes, 'You don't know what you are missing, and I want to be the one to change your mind.' So they go for it. But I think that's naive and narcissistic, because the gay men I know have been gay and out for a long time and are comfortable with their sexuality."

But Ann's sort of common-sense realism doesn't stop some women from having their moments of romantic infatuation or fantasy about their gay friends. Jacquie says of her long-time friend Carlton, "There was a period at the beginning when I had a crush on him in a way that really didn't disturb me very much. I just allowed myself to fantasize, 'Someday I'll marry Carl,' but naturally I never brought it up with him. *He* said once, 'You know, *we* should go to Italy together. I would love to show you Florence.' And I said over the lunch table, 'Oh Carl, I can't tell you what it does to me when you say that.' He just threw his head back and laughed. Luckily, it never created the slightest tension between us, and I never felt he drew away from me. But still I did notice that the conversation didn't continue after that and the whole subject was dropped."

Lily, whose friendship with her friend Marcus dates back to their time in college together, confessed to similar feelings. "I did have a crush on Marcus. I thought for a while there (especially if I had had a couple of drinks at a party we had gone to together), 'Oh, you know, gee, could anything ever happen?' But even when I thought that, it was always with the awareness that it wouldn't, couldn't, and probably shouldn't. He, of course, never did anything to lead me to believe it would be different between us. So with Marc, I think my feelings were due to that wonderful freedom and depth we could have together." Lily continued, "And that is one thing I do love about being with my gay friends: the opportunity to be affectionate or even flirtatious without worrying about its going anywhere. There is real freedom with that. Being with them is a safe space that is really quite wonderful. We can play, goof off, have fun, and joke and not worry about how it will be taken."

Each of the women who did fall in love or who entertained various romantic fantasies about their gay male friends handled the situation in her own way. Some like Jacquie never talked about them explicitly, whereas others, like Harriet, were very open about it to their gay friends. When asked what she had done with her feelings of attraction toward her gay friends, Harriet told Rob matter-of-factly, "I talked about it and told them that I found them attractive. I have never had any problem with it. And you know, I have had gay men be very flirtatious with me. In fact, I was once in a situation where I did not have a reaction toward a particular gay man who was used to having women be attracted to him. And he got really annoyed with me. I wasn't flirting with him, because I thought in the situation it would have been very inappropriate. But he didn't like that very much. He had come to expect that sort of attention from women."

Other women, like Cynthia, handle their feelings, though, without discussing them. She recalled, "One gay man I worked with — who became a good friend of mine eventually — flirted with me a lot at the start. I really liked him, but I was getting really frustrated that he was flirting with me but then didn't ask me out. Plus, anytime I responded to the flirting he would back off. Well, then a coworker came to me and said, 'You know, Cyn, the only calls he ever gets are from men. I think you may have misinterpreted this.' And as it turns out, he was indeed gay, and he and I have been friends ever since. But I never confronted him about the flirting. He was really flirting, but to what end, I don't know.

I have no idea. I wasn't head over heels in love with him, but I was definitely interested."

While the majority of women we talked with have never fallen in love with their gay male friends, it is certainly understandable why some women would have feelings such as these women have expressed. What woman wouldn't be tempted by a wonderful, handsome, well-dressed, sensitive, talented, bright, and attentive gay male friend? More than one woman friend of Rob's has told him that she would gladly marry one of her gay friends, happy to trade off the sexual part of a marriage for a life with a man that so closely conforms to a romantic ideal of hers. However, since all the women who said this were in fact involved in good, solid, and long-term intimate relationships with male partners, Rob doubts whether such bold statements were meant seriously and suspects they were more akin to fantasizing aloud than meant to be taken literally.

Laura has her doubts whether Rob, ace interviewer, was entirely impartial when he elicited these stories from his interviewees: "I find it fascinating that so many of Rob's female friends had been in love with a gay man whereas none of my female friends ever have. Based on my own informal opinion poll, I discovered that most of my gay friends thought most women were secretly in love with them, whereas most straight women claimed they never entertained such thoughts. You do the math!"

For her part, Laura has never known a woman who would really entertain the prospect of marrying a gay man, and neither she nor any of her friends or acquaintances have ever fallen in love, or entertained romantic or sexual fantasies, about their gay friends. To do so would be a breach of their agreement, a real violation of an important boundary, akin to the gay man making unwanted sexual advances toward his female friend.

Laura observes, "I think that the concept of women falling in love with their gay friends is more of a stereotype than a reality. It assumes that the woman has no other love interest or isn't good enough, attractive enough, or interesting enough to have any other love interest. I also think that some gay men are expressing an unconscious but deep-rooted chauvinism when they assume women fall in love with gay men. Behind this idea is the wrong-headed assumption that women are so irrational and foolish they will fall helplessly in love with a man who can't respond in kind. Any woman worth her salt who has been involved in a close friendship with a gay man has learned one important lesson which my friend Patrick put very succinctly: 'Being gay doesn't necessarily have to do with who you can sleep with, it has to do with who you can fall in love with.' Once a woman really understands this simple truth, which I believe is key to understanding her gay friend, then she is much less likely to entertain romantic fantasies which can be so damaging to them both."

Laura's own experience has been very much in line with what women like Ann or Ellen, have expressed. Knowing that there was no possibility of either person falling in love with the other in a romantic way enabled her friendships to become very powerful and deep very quickly. Still, the reality of this permanent "unavailability" has also left a feeling of regret in some of the women we interviewed. Laura says, "I talked to so many women who told me that their friendships with gay men have "ruined them" for other men. I heard that one particular phrase a lot: "ruined" or "spoiled" them. There is a sadness, a melancholy, a longing that suddenly comes over them when they describe a man who is their soul mate but with whom they can never be romantically involved. It's not that they fantasize about being with their gay friends, or that they wish these men were straight – they really wouldn't change anything about their friends. It's more of a wish on the part of women that they could find someone straight they could love as easily, and the sadness comes with knowing that this may be an impossibility. And often this is something women feel they can't even discuss with their gay friend."

A similar feeling of regret occurs to gay men as well. Margaret told us of the time her best friend, Bob, a gay man, had arranged a party where she was finally going to meet his best childhood friend, a straight man, for the first time. The evening turned out to be particularly moving for Bob, who was able to introduce his two best friends to one another. Bob turned to Margaret and said, "This is so wonderful. The only thing that could make it better would be if I were your lover." He shared a similar emotion when his first boyfriend couldn't measure up to his best female friend, telling her, "You know, I think you and I have spoiled each other for other human beings." They both shared the joy of the friendship, but it was tempered by some regret. These two soulmates realized that, on the deepest level, there were things they would never be able to share.

Seeing the Dark Side

For the women who do have certain feelings about their gay friends but who hold such feelings to themselves, this lack of total honesty is for the most part understandable. To discuss openly whatever romantic notions they entertained about their gay friend would represent a tremendous risk with very little gain for them: given

"I used to lie awake in bed at night and feel bad about it because we were such good friends, and things went wrong. I felt used, and I also felt so remorseful about my behavior in the whole thing."

the situation, even in the best of circumstances, their romantic desires would be disappointed, and in the worst, they might even be ridiculed or rejected. So frequently nothing is said, as much to save themselves embarrassment as to spare their gay friend any sense that he was being pressured.

Nevertheless, most friends realize that many unspoken dynamics are going on under the surface.

The failure to communicate honestly can have unintended consequences, however, when a gay man is confronted with unwelcome romantic attention from a female friend. Adam, a very attractive actor, told us a story that illustrates the "dark side" of a woman's relationship to a gay man.

Adam is frequently cast in the role of a romantic leading man and thus gives off some serious "straight guy" energy. When he became friends with Peggy, a member of the crew on one of his shows and a woman with few friends and no romantic attachments, the relationship quickly became unhealthy. She offered to pick up his laundry, and without thinking, he took her up on it; after all, they had become good friends. She offered to housesit for him, and when he bought her a scarf to say thank you for housesitting, she gave him an intimate and expensive gift in return. When she came over to his house, she always managed to find excuses for spending the night there. The next day, she told everyone about it.

Adam became concerned when he heard from others that Peggy considered them more than just friends. Working on another show together, she began to talk about Adam to the other cast members as if he were her boyfriend. When he lost his apartment and stayed at her house, she led mutual friends to think he was sleeping with her in her room. After he quickly found his own place and moved out, Peggy left messages on his answering machine every day in an apparently obsessive attempt to establish a romantic relationship.

Like other gay men who had been in similar, although usually less extreme, situations with women, Adam was perplexed. Peggy had to know he was gay. Everyone knew. So why was she behaving this way? Adam faults himself for "continuing to do things I shouldn't have, things that made her think we had a relationship. In retrospect, I would have been clearer and not put myself in this situation. I was lazy — like when I moved in with her. It was the easiest thing to do at the time, and it was a big mistake. It allowed her to say we were living together."

Eventually, Adam confronted Peggy, sending her what he hoped was a clear message that he was uninterested and unhappy with her suggesting otherwise. "I said to her, 'Look, I'm gay. You know that

I'm gay, and I'm hearing from people that you are telling people that we have a relationship. And I want to be clear with you that I am your friend and that we have a friendship but nothing else.' I know that I wasn't particularly firm. I didn't say, 'Just stop all this.' Instead, I told her, 'I really like you, but I think your feelings about me are a lot stronger than mine are about you.'

Without a clear statement, however, Peggy's behavior continued to be a problem, leading Adam to ultimately break off their friendship. When he did so, Peggy didn't miss a beat, telling mutual friends and coworkers that "Adam broke up with me so he could explore his homosexuality." And while Peggy clearly had some problems taking "no" for an answer, Adam takes responsibility for not being active enough in setting limits when her unhealthy attachment first became apparent. Adam remembers, "I used to lie awake in bed at night and feel bad about it because we were such good friends, and things went wrong. I felt used, and I also felt so remorseful about my behavior in the whole thing. It's easy to make this story anecdotal and to make her seem twisted and psycho. But I constantly have to remind myself how much responsibility I had in the unhealthiness and the dependence in the relationship, and how much I fed it and subconsciously chose it. In retrospect, I think I should have been harsher in saying 'no.'"

Obviously both participants in this story abused their "friendship" and must bear responsibility for the destructiveness of their relationship. But there is something about the friendship between a gay man and a straight woman that sometimes permits such an attachment to take root. When a woman has an obsessive desire for a straight man, it is quickly put to the test: either he will sleep with her or he won't, and that decides the question. But with a gay man, a woman may have a built-in excuse for why he's not with her at that moment. He's "exploring his homosexuality" or only "temporarily gay," but she can delude herself that he will eventually come around and become her lover in the future. And as we saw from this story, while a straight man would probably be more definitive and forceful in telling this woman to back off, a gay man might question whether such a confrontation was necessary, particularly when he *knew* she was aware of his homosexuality.

And it is stories like Adam and Peggy's that makes straight women afraid to tell their gay friends about any feelings they might have for them. As Josie admitted to us, "I don't want my gay friends to think I'm some sort of stalker, or some obsessive woman who has no straight men in her life and therefore attaches herself to them as a substitute. These men may be gay, but I still want them to think well of me – and I frankly don't think any men, gay or straight, think well of women who are summarily rejected by other men or who pine away for men who aren't interested in them. If I were ever attracted to a gay friend, I would definitely keep it to myself."

Does such a lack of frankness harm a friendship? Would it be better to make a clean breast of it all and just put it out on the table? For the few and the brave who had in fact chosen to do that with their gay male friends, the results depended, expectably, on the people involved. Lottie, for example, being an upfront kind of lady, simply told her friend that she was developing a whole set of physical feelings toward him, despite the fact that both of them were with other partners, and the discussion in a certain way brought them closer. Lottie told us, "He listened to me and wasn't defensive or anything. So talking about it made it even clearer to me why I loved him so much and why he was so special. I mean, it's a real friend you can talk to about everything, and he was really one of my closest."

Most of these friendships could probably survive a discussion of this sort. But to discuss the issue of being in love is difficult for other reasons and has less to do with the particularities of these specific sorts of friendships and more with the general dynamics of "being in love."

Psychologically speaking, "being in love" is a delusional state, in which only the most idealized aspects of an individual are seen and responded to, while the remaining aspects are screened out of consciousness, set aside, ignored or rejected as not real. It is a one-sided perception of someone, almost always supported by a lack of familiarity with that person. You fall in love across a crowded room, at first sight, in an instant. In other words, you always fall in love with someone you don't really know, and as nearly all of us can attest, once you get to know the person better, spending time with him or her, that wonderful initial glow can begin to fade. Familiarity breeds balance, if not contempt.

Being in love is seductive for many, many reasons. The one-sided perception of only ideal characteristics of another person promises to make life simple and joyful, and naturally, this rosy picture produces an extremely pleasurable state of ongoing excitement. It is a diet of emotional sugar uncut by the salt of conflicts, the sourness of failure, and the bitterness of disappointment. Yet, very much like a diet of pure sweets, being in love does not really provide what we need to grow fully and healthfully into our own selves or into relationships with others. Why is this? Because people are not made up of exclusively ideal aspects. Each of us has our weaknesses, wounds, brokenness, and shadows, and so, contrary to having a real relationship with an actual person, when one is in love with someone, one is actually ignoring the true person in favor of an unreal image.

The ancients knew that this state of being in love was bad news. People in classical Rome did just about anything to make sure that the fearsome goddess of love, Venus, would not pay attention to them. The absolute last thing that they wanted was for Venus to send her uncontrollable brat of a son, Cupid, to attack them with his arrows, whose poisoned tips would surely ruin their sanity and life. The mythology of love, watered down into the form we see in contemporary Valentine's Day cards, was seen in a very different way back then: being in love was seen as the result of an act of divine aggression, a sickness, and a pathology from which weak people did not recover and which often brought down even the strongest women and men. Remember, to be "smitten" is to be hit. Surely we all have experienced this dark side of being in love — the heartsickness and exhaustion of it, the unfulfillability of our desires, the mad all-absorbing quality of it. And if any proof is needed of its destructiveness, contemporary events show us that kings and presidents as well as common people will throw away power, money, fame and future when seized with this state of idealization.

Thus, when straight women fall in love with gay men, one has to wonder. Not to judge, far from it. But it is suspicious, especially when one notices that such an essential part of gay men's experiences — their sexuality — tends to be excluded from the conversation. And yet, the net result of these relationships is so positive, so grounding, so loving — could it be that something else is going on here on the romantic or sexual level? Having looked at the double-edged sword of idealization between gay men and straight women, another psychological dynamic might also be occurring: namely, projection.

Projection's Place

Freud put forth the notion of projection as a defensive mechanism, a way that we protect ourselves from feeling things about ourselves that elicit anxiety or discomfort. If we are angry with someone but have been told that it isn't nice to be angry, many of us instead of feeling our own anger will instead perceive the other person as being angry at us. (And of course, voicing our opinion to the other person, who may not feel angry at all initially, almost always guarantees that our projection will become reality, since no one really likes to be told what he or she is feeling.) Nevertheless, all of us at one time or another manage to rid ourselves of troublesome feelings through projection.

Being in love, as we all know, requires no such work — it just magically happens. But love, real love, real acceptance, real knowledge of another person — now that is a different story.

C. G. Jung, however, took Freud's ideas of projection and developed a different set of ideas about it. Rather than seeing projection as a defense against unwanted feelings, Jung noted how universal the tendency to project was for human beings. He theorized that such a universal tendency could not merely be a defense but that projection also had a positive function psychologically. Projection brings two people together: you can't very well attribute your feelings to someone else if there is no someone to project onto. Projection, therefore, is more often than not at the heart of an attraction two people feel toward each other.

Moreover, Jung pointed out, if you are aware of this from the start, if you let yourself consider the fact that much of what you think you know about someone else you just met is really just a set of your own projections, then the relationship gives you a unique and wonderful opportunity to widen your own consciousness of yourself. Why? Because if you are indeed projecting, then what you see in the other person can only be unowned aspects of your own personality. In other words, Jung thought projection was one of the primary ways we human beings come in contact with and begin to see the unconscious, unappreciated, and unintegrated aspects of our own personality.

Needless to say, this is good news and bad news. The good news, according to Jung, is that our relationships help us to discover who we really are and to come into our own wholeness as individuals. The bad news is, because much of the initial misperceptions of the other person need to be seen as such — misperceptions, projections, fantasies and delusions — a good relationship of whatever sort requires that we do the hard work of owning our own stuff. Being in love, as we all know, requires no such work — it just magically happens. But love, real love, real acceptance, real knowledge of another person — now *that* is a different story. Love takes time. Love takes patience. Love means work. And when people insist on confusing "being in love" with love, it's quite understandable. Who wouldn't like it to be so?

But looking on the bright side: if Jung is right, then the very projections that bring two people together initially — as lovers or as friends — need to be carefully examined because in those misperceptions are elements of our own personality. If we see our projections as opportunities, chances to grow in awareness and depth, then indeed "falling in love" is in fact very good news indeed.

So what is it that women are seeing in their gay male friends that lead them to fall in love with them? What is going on when Jacquie, for example, finds herself with a crush on her friend Carlton, or when Cynthia perceives her gay coworker as flirting with her? Rather than pathologize or denigrate these perceptions, Jung would suggest that women are projecting certain elements of their own unconscious male side onto these men. We find this perspective a far more intriguing thought and certainly worth trying on for size.

What if all the wonderful things we have heard thus far from the women we spoke to about their gay friends were, to some degree, actually projections? What if Jacquie is describing her own romantic nature when her friend Carlton's suggestion of going to Paris makes her head spin a bit? What if it is Lily's own flirtatiousness and sensuality she is perceiving in her coworker's behavior? If Jung is correct, then these women are getting glimpses of their own male side, a certain kind of masculinity that only their gay male friends can carry for them in projected form — a romantic, tender, respectful masculinity, a masculinity their straight male partners and friends do not incarnate for them, a maleness largely devoid of needless aggression, a fluid and sometimes androgynous manliness.

And might it not also be that gay men find themselves so consistently drawn toward their straight female friends on the basis of certain projections as well? Is the reason so many gay men refrain from talking about sex with their women friends because they screen out their own very male phallic energy from these friendships? Do they do this in order to live out a certain kind of femininity that is not given much space in the culture at large, a femininity that is even less acceptable in the current cult of hypermasculinity that has seized the gay male community in the past two decades? When Laura's gay friends spend so much time, energy and attention making sure *she* looks her best, fussing about *her* clothes, *her* highlights or the lighting in *her* apartment, are they not actually living out certain aspects of their own femininity through her? Women friends may allow gay men to put aside the sometimes overwhelming demands of masculinity and to touch, enjoy, and revel in their own femininity, just as gay men may give women a very special space to contact

that lovely, fine, tender masculinity that character-
izes their own souls, a masculinity that women, and
only women, can incarnate.

If we look at these issues in this constructive
way, noting the idealizations, projections, inclu-
sions, and omissions, then we see once again what
many of us already know: the friendship between
gay men and straight women provides each of the
friends with unique opportunity to project out and,
potentially, to integrate a maleness and a femaleness like no other relationships can. With their
women friends, gay men have something that cannot
be found with other gay men — their female friends
give them respite from sexuality and thus the opportunity to be everything they are, with no single
aspect of their personalities overshadowing the others. And the straight women in these friendships
find something similar, something not often, if ever
really, found in a heterosexual relationship — a
home for their whole selves, a place of freedom and
relaxation from what is "masculine" and "feminine"
for a change, a place of acceptance.

In this way, the friendships between gay men
and straight women represent what Rebecca Nahas
and Myra Turley way back in 1979 called "the new

couple," a relationship that they felt heralded a new era in male-female relationships.[6] For our part, almost twenty years later, we would say the era of the "new couple" has come into its own.

9. Dealing with People's Reactions

 Of all the things we learned while talking to people about their friendships, one of the most perplexing was the extent to which the relationships between gay men and straight women are marginalized, discounted and disparaged, even sometimes by the friends themselves. When people asked what sort of project we were working on, they often laughed nervously when we told them, making it clear that this did not seem

Why do so many people attach some level of unimportance to these relationships, and why can they engender outright hostility from those who do not participate in them?

to them a serious topic for discussion. Others indicated that they found such friendships unacceptable: what was wrong with a woman that she needed to hang around with gay men, and why can't gay men just hang out with each other?

As shows like *Will & Grace* reach a wide and mainstream audience, including the parents and boyfriends of the straight women and gay men it portrays, it is certain to increase understanding, and hopefully acceptance, of the friendship. But this is not to say that the relationship has been "mainstreamed" by all the media attention. Discussions of this friendship are still very much the exception to the romance-focused rules governing our culture. And however willing audiences may be to accept such friendship among sophisticated New Yorkers on sitcoms, the real-life loved ones of these friends may still view it with suspicion, or ignore it as entirely insignificant. Why do so many people attach some level of unimportance to these relationships or ignore them entirely, and why do these frienships engender outright hostility from those who do not participate in them?

As we have said, one of our prime motivations for exploring this topic was our wish to affirm the value and indispensability of such relationships, so coming to appreciate the extent to which popular culture and various individuals slighted and thought poorly of these friendships took us back some. At that point, we began to ask ourselves a different question: "How *do* others really see the relationship between gay men and straight women?"

So we asked the people we interviewed how other people in their lives — boyfriends, partners, family, and other friends — had reacted to their friendship. Had they experienced support and celebration from other people in their lives? Or had family, friends and partners expressed negative attitudes toward these friendships? Naturally, we got an earful.

Family Dynamics

When it came to family members' attitudes toward these friendships, some stories had a positive tone. Ann, for example, accompanied her gay friend Brad on house-hunting excursions with Brad's father. "I went around with his Dad as if Brad and I were going to buy the house together. At least that's what it felt like, like his Dad would approve more if I were there. He had been so difficult about it, but then Brad invited me along and his father really changed. We went to brunch together and he was in a whole other mood. Suddenly, it was like there's Brad with his girlfriend, as if we were buying the house together."

The friendship between the two of them helped to make a difficult situation a little easier for everyone.

Brad's take on this incident was a little different, but essentially the same. He remembered, "When Ann came with me that Sunday, it made things so much easier. My father had had a tough time accepting that I was gay, and I wasn't entirely sure I could count on him for help to buy the house I wanted. But he really responded to Ann, whether it was flirtation or just happy that I had such a decent, sweet friend, or a mixture of both. I think his seeing my friendship with her reassured him I could have a normal life — something he was worried about, with my being gay and out about it."

Whether Ann helped provide an illusion of heterosexuality to the situation for Brad's father, making him feel more comfortable with Brad's decision to buy a house, or whether Brad's father was reassured by his son's close friendship, it is hard to say. But the gist of the story was that the whole situation felt good – the friendship between the two of them helped to make a difficult situation a little easier for everyone.

Other women told us stories of being taken aside by their gay friend's mother in order to be quietly told, just in case she didn't know it, that her gay friend was "not marriage material." Pamela, for example, was cornered in the kitchen (a favorite ambush spot) by her gay friend's mother who expressed regret that she was never going to be her daughter-in-law but who assured her that she would "always be a part of the family." And some parents can be altogether hilarious when they "double date" with a gay man and his female friend. Josie reported an evening out at dinner during which her friend's father constantly complimented her on her appearance, elbowed his son in the rib cage, and urged him to join in the compliments toward her, while winking at them both suggestively. These family members are well-intentioned but appear to be laboring under the misapprehension that their gay son could "turn straight" if the woman would just, as one mother suggested to Laura, "wear something a little lower cut."

However, some mothers persist in denying their gay son's homosexuality by pretending that his female friends are his girlfriends — sending them gifts, including them in family celebrations and treating them, for all intents and purposes, as daughters-in-law. Margaret told us about being a part of her gay best friend's family: "I think sometimes it was a little bit convenient for him. I was like the girlfriend. I was the date for every wedding. I went to the birthday and anniversary parties, the barbecues, and I think it did keep people off his back." Other family members, though, particularly older relatives, just don't seem to notice the "gay thing" at all. Laura certainly wouldn't have expected her grandmother, who vehemently denied that Liberace was gay to her dying day, to believe that any of Laura's handsome friends were "that way." Cathie was surprised during our interview to hear Matt tell the story of her wedding reception, during which an older relative of hers pulled Matt aside and told him, "Too bad, you waited too long."

Then there were stories in which certain family members quietly disapproved of these friendships on the grounds that their daughters, nieces or cousins were "wasting their time" hanging around with a bunch of gay men during their peak years of eligibility. The mothers of a number of the gay men we interviewed worried about their sons' female friends : Did these women realize their son was gay? Was he sure they knew? Why were these women still hanging around?

Unfortunately, however, we sometimes heard stories of more overt familial conflicts arising around these friendships, as with Ingrid and Kenneth. Ingrid told us, "The two of us have never actually had any conflict or breakdown of communication, not even really any serious misunderstanding. The one situation where there was some conflict, however, was around his sister who felt threatened by me because she depended so much on Kenneth. For a while she was envious of our friendship, and she turned very negative toward me. It got to the point where I couldn't go over and visit if she were there. She managed to finally work through her jealousy and we get along fine now, but for about a year and a half, things were very tense and it affected my friendship with Kenneth."

Such stories show how certain families struggle for a long time to accept their sons and daughters, brothers and sisters, as they really are. Whether funny, disturbing or touching, these family stories highlight how important the love and acceptance is between the two friends and make clear why such friendships are so valuable.

The Jealous Boyfriend

Personal jealousy is the theme here, and this jealousy is very often present when a boyfriend is confronted with a gay man who is close, maybe closer than he is, to his girlfriend. Cynthia told us, for example, "Some of my heterosexual male friends have had difficulties with the fact that I have gay friends. I don't think so much because they are gay, per se, but the men get jealous of the relationship, the fact that I am so close to these guys. Many straight men don't like gay men, period, but in my experience, the difficulty is that the straight men are jealous of the closeness I have with my gay male friends. For example, a guy I dated made a comment about Dave, my mahjongg

This guy doesn't care "how gay this friend of yours claims he is." An intruder is invading the boyfriend's territory and needs to back off.

partner, 'You guys are such good friends,' which he said in a way that made it clear he was upset about how close we were. So I said to him, 'You know, Dave and I have been friends a long time. It has nothing to do with you.' He was clearly jealous of the friendship, in my opinion." Cynthia went on, "Another boyfriend I had once really disliked one of my gay friends, and not for any reason I could understand. There was really no good reason for him to harbor that level of dislike. Again it was jealousy. He'd have never copped to it, of course, and frankly, I don't think it was homophobia, because this guy had gay friends himself he worked with closely. In fact I had met him through a gay friend. He was just jealous of my friendship."

Harriet, with a thoughtfulness quite characteristic of her, sheds some light on a possible reason that such jealousy from straight boyfriends exists. "My relationship with Martin is the deepest friendship I have with a man, outside of my partner. I don't know if such a close friendship would be possible with a straight man because straight men, generally, do not allow this kind of depth without a sexual relationship. A straight man *wants* to have that erotic spark with a woman."

In other words, some of these women's heterosexual male partners envy the closeness and simply cannot imagine that such intimacy between a man and woman can exist without that "erotic spark" being there. Cynthia says as much when she notes, "A lot of straight men are very unclear about what it means to be gay. They think that 'gay' means that they hit on women sometimes or a woman could turn him straight. Who knows what they are thinking? The fact is, I don't really think about my friends being gay. I think about them as friends, and I don't really think about them being gay or straight. It's pretty secondary to me, at least in my conscious thinking. However, I do have a lot of friendships with gay men, and they are among the closest friendships I have. It's just a lot easier than with straight men. It's really hard to be good friends with a straight man. The friendships I do have with straight men are limited: either they are mostly work-related or they are with ex-boyfriends. In either case, they are very limited and not what I would call close."

Other men may be threatened by the closeness itself, and feel excluded by it. Ross, who had thought about this issue a fair bit, gave us his theory.

"I think straight men are afraid of gay men. They're afraid they won't measure up. In a way, straight men look at their girlfriends as sharing certain things only with their own girlfriends — that all women understand each other. Straight men consider gay men more like a girlfriend's girlfriends emotionally. I think men are afraid of women, because they don't understand them. They are emotional, and straight men are not as emotional. I know some who are, but those would be my favorite straight men."

And of course, there is the boyfriend who may react on a more basic level, who doesn't like *any* other man getting that close to his girlfriend, especially one who is good looking, intelligent and articulate, and one whom she obviously adores. This guy doesn't care "how gay this friend of yours claims he is." An intruder is invading the boyfriend's territory and needs to back off.

Needless to say, a gay man's boyfriend may have similar feelings of possessiveness or territoriality toward his lover's female friends, though the tone of the jealousy is a bit different. Lowell told us that his own long-term partner often rolls his eyes and makes snide comments when Lowell is going out to lunch or to the opera with a female friend. "I don't know if he is jealous or threatened, so to speak. He knows there's nothing going on between my girl-friends and me that would get between us. I get more the feeling he feels left out or excluded." However, Lowell laughed. "I invite him to come along — my female friends all think the world of him — but he's a stick-in-the-mud, so if he feels left out, it's his own fault. And you'd think he'd be more inclined to feel this when I go out with my gay male friends, but he doesn't. It's only with my women friends I get this reaction from him."

What all these stories indicate to us is that the partner's jealousy comes directly out of a very accurate perception of just how unique and special such friendships are. These friendships provide something that the primary relationship can't, and a partner's reaction of possessiveness or support, understanding or competition, most certainly does not go unnoticed.

Here Comes Homophobia

On top of the personal jealousy, envy and competitiveness that arise toward these friendships, a different brand of negative attitude comes out that is

more explicitly homopho-
bic. Ingrid put it quite
plainly when she told us,
"If I have friends that
don't get along well with
my gay friends, I see less
of them. I had one woman
friend who became Roman
Catholic. We had a conversation one day where I
said, if the political
stresses in my church led
to people taking sides in a
public way about homo-
sexuality, I would have to
take the side of gay peo-
ple. That is where I would

*Some family
members,
particularly the
parents of straight
women who have a
lot of gay friends,
worry that these
friendships mask her
own, hidden,
homosexuality, a
sexuality the parents
would find totally
unacceptable.*

pitch my tent. I would be committed to that. She
responded abruptly, 'Well, I'd be on the other side.'
And at that point I didn't know if she and I would go
on being friends or not. I still care a lot about her
and feel warmly toward her, as long as we can stay
clear of a polarizing discussion about that issue. It
makes me sad when I notice that sort of close-mind-
edness in friends."

Several of the gay men we talked to reported losing female friends when these friends became active in certain conservative religious groups, felt pressure from other "friends" or neighbors to look unfavorably on homosexuality, or when they married men who had negative attitudes toward gay people. From a different direction, some family members, particularly the parents of straight women who have a lot of gay friends, worry that these friendships mask her own, hidden, homosexuality, a sexuality the parents would find totally unacceptable.

Concerning parental reactions, Meredith told us this story. "My parents treated me like, if I was single, didn't have kids, and didn't have a man, then I was nothing. I have a great job in publishing, but my parents think I work in a bookstore. They have no idea what I do, and they make no effort to find out. One weekend I went home to visit, and we started arguing late into the night about gays in the military, which my father is totally against. And he got madder and madder. And I wondered, why? Finally it became clear that he was convinced I was a lesbian, because all of my friends are gay, and my parents had been wanting to ask but were afraid to. So finally he yelled it at me, at four in the morning,

"Are you gay?" I said no. There was a brief moment when I hesitated — let's put that grandkid thing to bed right now — but I said no. And I told them that there were a lot of gay men I was really close to, and that I hated it when they said these things, when they made jokes, when they talked negatively about them."

Meredith paused before continuing. "No matter what I said to my father, though, he just kept saying, 'All your friends are freaks,' over and over. 'All your friends are freaks' because they're not this way or that. And I would say, 'All my friends are not freaks. They are people who care about me. And they take good care of me.' And I had to make it very clear to them that I had no problem with what anybody does and I didn't know why they did. After that, their attitude toward my best friend Dale, who was gay, became more positive. In fact, when I was in a bad car accident, my father came up to me and said, 'You can rely on Dale more than you can rely on any person you've ever known.' And it's not because he's gay, it's because he's a good person."

Some straight husbands express their own homophobia by concocting "good reasons" why their wives need to offload their gay friends. Although the end of the friendship may not ever be articulated, the woman suddenly disappears from her gay friend's life. Alex, who works in the fashion industry, tells this story. "Several straight women friends have fallen out of my life when they got married. These friends were very close to me, but after they got married, I stopped hearing from them. For example, Sally, who I worked with at my first real job, was kind of a soul mate to me. We were very much alike in our likes and our tastes and our attitudes toward life — that laid-back, easy sort of thing. She and I look alike, and people always asked if we were brother and sister. I don't have any sisters and I felt like an older brother to her. I was always very protective of her in that way, and we stayed very close. And for her wedding, I was there about her dress, about her flowers — I even registered her — she wouldn't have done that without me. We did lots of things together, but then as soon as she got married — all of a sudden, nothing."

Their experience, sadly, is a common one for all friends, but in the case of these friendships, a new husband may have an especially hard time accepting his new wife's gay friends. As Alex reflects further on what happened with Sally. "One reason may be her husband. I don't think he's comfortable around me. I don't think any man is going to be comfortable around a really good looking single man who's friends with his wife, no matter what. I don't like him because I think he's not good enough for her; I don't think he appreciates her the way she should be appreciated. I think at this time in Sally's life, she just decided she wanted to get married. And she just went for it, at the cost of our friendship."

The homophobic quality of some people's envy is more overt and pronounced, as in Debra's story. "I am in theatre and was hired as a dancer in a touring musical. Generally, when you are on the road, you forge these great friendships. I would have loved to have had a good girlfriend on tour, but in this company all the girls were either married or they didn't have room to accept a close friend. So the people that I happened to bond with were all gay men. One day, we were all together, hanging out, and the one straight guy in the company said to me, 'Oh you, you're just part of the gay mafia,' with the implication that he thought we were privileged or got special treatment. So when I asked him what he meant, he said, 'You and your friends are just like the gay mafia and you are the gay mafia princess.'

One of Debra's gay friends from the road, Donald, heard the same things. "People think there's a gay mafia in show business, but I don't think it's real. What they really mean is that there is a clique. I don't think there is some vast gay mafia, but people have to find some reason to explain why they are not getting hired. I guess, for those people, life is just an extension of bad high school experiences."

This idea of a "gay Mafia" with its distinctly envious overtones is really simply one of the more sophisticated ways to stereotype and discriminate against gay men. Indeed, George Weinberg, who more or less launched the term "homophobia" into popular culture back in 1973 with his book *Society and The Healthy Homosexual*, lists "envy" as one of the prime forces behind the fear and hatred of homosexuals, and this envy is often expressed as a perception of hostility on the part of gay people who are perceived and characterized as "militant," "angry," or "subversive." Perhaps such fear and hatred is to be expected from certain straight men who enjoy many social privileges and benefits of being in control but who are excluded from friendships between gay men and straight women. Thus, their response can be to characterize gay men and their friends as a monolithic conspiracy with hostile, subversive intentions. Here we see the psychological dynamic of projection once again: it is not gay people who run some sort of unified mafia hostile to straight men, but quite the contrary, it is these straight men who feel threatened and hostile toward gay men and their friends.

Debra's and Donald's stories, with their description of the attitudes shown toward their friendship, is sadly ironic: even in fields like the arts — where gay men's contributions are notable and have long history — prejudice and stereotyping may still rear their ugly heads.

Whether it is homophobia, familial disapproval, the ignorance or intolerance of friends and neighbors, or the insecurity of boyfriends and husbands, the friendships may be disparaged or even ignored by many of those whom we are close to. With a deeply ingrained belief that there is something fundamentally lacking, or even wrong, with the relationship and with those who participate in it, what we've found is that all of this hatred and prejudice gets summed up in a single, pernicious stereotype: the fag hag.

10. Defending Each Other: Fag Hags and Other Stereotypes

Of all the manifesta-tions of hostility toward straight women's friend-ships with gay men, the most obvious and offensive is the use of the derisive term "fag hag." As Rob found while working on this book, this phrase was so

Some people found it impossible to imagine that the "fag hag phenomenon" wasn't going to be the central focus of the book.

inextricably entwined with the very concept of the friendship between gay men and straight women, some people found it impossible to imagine that the "fag hag phenomenon" wasn't going to be the central focus of the book. "Over the months during our research and before we came up with a title for this book, it seemed like I was trapped in one of those science fiction stories, where the unlucky hero, for reasons known only to the author, is condemned to repeat the same event again and again and again, in an endless time warp. The scenario would always go something like this:

"Friend, acquaintance, or curiosity seeker: 'So, what are you working on? Another book?' I'd respond, 'Yeah. My co-author and I are going to be writing a book on the friendship between gay men and straight women.' The other person would then say, 'And what's the title going be?' (snicker, snicker.) "*Fag Hags*?""

"I mounted a variety of responses to this dubious quip. At first, I managed a weak smile, the sort Miss Manners recommends when you want to politely show disapproval and offense without sinking to overt rudeness yourself. Unfortunately, that rarely did the trick, because usually the response I then got was a sort of insistent gush. "That's too bad. I mean, what else could you call it? It's got to be called "*Fag Hags*." Then I would explain, trying not to sound too patronizing, that we intended to focus on the *positive* aspects of the friendships between gay men and straight women, so really that title didn't suit the book we wanted to write. And I would then, strangely, have to deal with my interlocutor's disappointment.

"After about six such conversations, I became more confrontational. 'Actually,' I'd say, only half-facetiously, 'we are banning that phrase from the book altogether. The expression "fag hag" is not going to appear anywhere in the book.' Reactions to this bit of hyperbole ranged from incredulous to chastened. 'Why?' was the usual question."

Why, indeed?

The Charming Epithet

There are a few phrases in English that do a certain kind of double duty as insults. "White trash" is one, for example, serving as a backhanded racial slur at blacks while simultaneously insulting the economically disadvantaged folks to which it overtly refers. "Fag hags" is like that; it derides both the woman as a "hag" and her acquaintances as "fags." It is not a description any woman aspires to hear applied to her. Among people who do not enjoy such a friendship, it is generally an insult, a put-down used to describe the stereotype of an unattractive woman forced to socialize with gay men because other, ostensibly

While the phrase clearly didn't apply to them or to their friends, they could all spot a "fag hag" when they saw one.

more worthwhile, men shun her. The sting of being called a fag hag is so palpable that some women told us that they actually went out of their way at one time in their lives not to socialize too much with gay men, lest they be labeled as such.

To those who use the term as an insult, it is not enough to be homophobic: you must add a dash of class-conscious snobbism to your bigotry as well. Accordingly, you are not at risk of being called a "fag hag" if you hang around with a gay man who is your hairdresser, decorator or other "service provider." The "help" can be of low moral character, but your personal friends must always be "our kind of people." Nor are you a "fag hag" if you consort with a gay coworker. You don't get to pick who you work with, after all. But if you dare choose a gay man as a personal friend, well, then, you may very well be labeled with this charming epithet.

In the interest of fairness, however, when it comes to using the term "fag hag," we do need to acknowledge that there are differing views on this term held by the very gay men and straight women who enjoy these friendships. Some brag about it. Madonna recently gave an interview in connection with her upcoming film about a woman and her gay best friend in which she proudly described herself as "a big fag hag."

But most surprising to us was the consensus of opinion among straight women and their gay male friends that, while the phrase clearly didn't apply to them or to their friends, they could all spot a "fag hag" when they saw one. One person said, "It's a 1970s concept of people on the party circuit — Bianca or Liza hanging out with Halston at Studio 54." Another summed it up in this way: "A fag hag is someone who lives vicariously through a gay existence. She goes to the gay bars with gay guys and is involved in all their relationships and their rituals." One of Laura's friends told her, "There is a fag hag extreme. I know women who stopped having relationships with men or who didn't pursue them because they were having relationships with gay men. I know some gay men who would leech onto that type of person and have a relationship where neither side could get the sexual satisfaction but would get the emotional satisfaction. It's negative if you put all your eggs in one basket, that is, if people limit themselves to only that type of relationship."

The "fag hags" we hear described are women who hang out with gay men most, if not all, of the time; who frequent gay bars as primary social outlets for themselves; who have gone through obsessive-compulsive relationship after relationship with gay man after gay man, continuing to believe that she will "turn" the next one she pursues. They may also be described as women who shrink from a fuller heterosexual relationship due to neurotic fear and anxiety and who take refuge in a circle of far more limited relationships with gay men.

An extreme example may be found in the protagonist of Robert Rodi's 1993 novel *Fag Hag*. Natalie is an obsessive woman who tries to poison all her gay friend's romances, and the author's description of her in the opening of his book typifies the negative, and some would say hostile, stereotype so associated with a fag hag:

"Natalie Stathis moussed her hair until it stood straight up and resembled a henna-rinsed mushroom cloud. She applied more makeup than a vision-impaired Las Vegas showgirl, and put on the new smock-like Claude Montana frock that Peter said made her look like a hand puppet, forcing her to say 'Fuck you' and hit him in the arm and pretend not to mind. Her wrists jangled with bracelets, all of them cheap and gaudy, although her ears were set with real diamonds — nine of them. And as she tagged along while Peter made his usual Saturday night rounds of Chicago's gay bars and discos, she beamed a smile that pleaded, 'Notice me!' She pressed herself, all hundred and seventy-odd pounds, through crowds of taut, muscular young men and, through sheer flamboyance, attracted the attention of a few of them. And as she talked to them, using every ounce of feminine wile and wit at her disposal, they laughed in delight and flattered her and sometimes even kissed her, but never, never once, not even for a moment, did they stop looking over her shoulder for something better."[7]

The multiplicity of insults in this description would never be tolerated were they leveled at a racial or ethnic minority. We heard the term "fag hag" from people of different races and religions, from both the highly educated and sophisticated to the more homespun and intuitive people we talked to. What is it about gay men and the straight women who love them that permits this stereotype to flourish, even among so-called enlightened people?

The Power of Insult

As with all insults that rely on stereotypes, when the word "fag hag" is tossed about, the slur reaches beyond the particular and paints a whole group in pejorative colors. So what exactly makes this insult an insult? What assumptions, expectations and prejudices lie beneath this slur? In a way, insults of this type are negative in the sense of a photographic negative. They reveal their opposite: the heavy weight of social

Behind the definition of a woman as a "hag" — fag or otherwise — is the hidden, sexist assumption that a woman's worth as a woman is to be determined or defined on the basis of her relationship to heterosexual men.

expectations forced upon women — and men — in our culture.

For women, the term "fag hag" makes clear that it is a cardinal sin to be unattractive — though what "attractive" might be (at any given moment, in any given situation, in the eye of any given beholder) is open to endless speculation. One gay man was brutally frank about his idea of the connection between unattractiveness and the definition of a "fag hag." He told us, "A fag hag is the type of person who doesn't take care of herself, or who has been told she's unattractive. She's not the prom queen. It comes from lack of self-confidence. She's let herself go or put on a lot of weight, and suddenly she gets all this attention from a gay man; or else it's a gay man in the same situation getting a lot of attention from a woman.

Usually, in discussions of physical beauty, certain ideal standards are referred to, but these are exceedingly vague — a range of weight, a size of breast, a shape of body, a color of skin. In reality, there are no objective standards but merely individual, subjective responses on the part of individual people to other individual people. Nevertheless, women tend to strive endlessly to achieve some absolute standard, basing their aspirations on images encountered in the media or on images encountered in the heads of the various men they come into contact with. And to be "unattractive" is not OK. It puts you in a different group. You are no longer a "woman." You have become a "hag."

Yet this begs the question: attractive to whom? "Attractive" is an adjective that requires an object. To whom? Well, "attractive" to straight men is the obvious answer. And here we see that behind the definition of a woman as a "hag" — fag or otherwise — is the hidden, sexist assumption that a woman's worth as a woman is to be determined or defined on the basis of her relationship to heterosexual men. If she attracts them, then she has achieved woman-hood in this universe of standards created by and for heterosexual men; if not, then she is a creature of another sort, not really a woman. She is a "hag."

Another common piece of this stereotype, we found, was that most people almost always described a "fag hag" as overweight. To many heterosexual men, including those who are overweight themselves, a "fat chick" is one of the worst things you can be. This bit of chauvinism appears to have been adopted by many gay men as well, who often feel the need to explain why their female friends are still single by referring to their weight. Of course, volumes and volumes on women and weight have been written from every imaginable perspective — feminist, sociological, psychological, anthropological, even biological — most of them revealing that the obsession with female thinness in American culture is a complex knot, in part a gender-role double standard (men are "big" while women are "small"), in part a means of social control (thin women can "control" their bodies, fat women are "out of control" and thus possibly "uncontrollable") and in part, a symbol of power (fat historically representing fertility and appetite in a woman, qualities certain men find threatening). That "fag hags" should almost universally be portrayed as fat — Madonna notwithstanding — makes sense in this context; they are women who have chosen a different path than the conventional models of relationship would have them choose.

This one uncomfortable feature of the "fag hag" myth may have, nevertheless, some tenuous connection to reality. We spoke to several women who were extremely unhappy with their weight and who admitted to seeking out gay men as a refuge from the harsher judgments of straight men. Margaret, a vivacious, if unconventional, beauty, spoke to us about a previous time in her life. She said, "When I went to gay bars and hung out with gay men, I was hiding in those relationships. I was very overweight and didn't feel so good about myself. I was terrified of straight men, which is one of the reasons I put the weight on, to push men away. But it felt like I could go out with a group of gay men, have a really good time, dance till I dropped, and not worry about it. And I used to hate going to straight bars, which were like a meat market. Nothing upset me more than going out and feeling like I couldn't dance at all because, after all, you didn't want to move your head, because you didn't want to mess your hair up, and you shouldn't sweat, because you didn't want to look bad, and you're trying to dance, but it felt like everyone was looking at you. Many times they'd put the dance floor down in a pit, and the railing at the top was surrounded by men, and I hated that. I just couldn't stand it. But I love to sweat, and I like to be sweating when I dance, and I love music, and my friend Bob is the same way. So I can go out with him and a couple of other friends, and it's terrific. And I can ask gay men to dance and they'll say yes – and

I would never ask a straight man to dance. So I guess that's what I mean when I say I was hiding from straight men with my gay friends."

Of course, beyond the weight issue, the term "hag" doesn't really simply denote "ugly" but also connotes a woman of a certain age, older than she "should be." A woman who has missed the boat. An old maid. And what's the problem with age? Well, the problem with age is again a hidden expectation of women that motherhood be the fulfillment of all they are and ever should be. Too old to be a mother is, like "unattractiveness," a cardinal sin. If you are too ugly to get a man in time to meet the social demand to reproduce and fulfill your femaleness, well, then, once again, your age has placed you in a different class. You are "less than" a normal woman.

Normal women have been made whole by the relationship to their husbands and the resulting children that issue from those marriages. If you are old and single, well, then you are not a woman but a "hag." This emphasis on procreative ability may well explain why the friendship between gay men and straight women is so marginalized: it is a relationship between men and women that blithely, and to some offensively, disregards the social mandate to create children.

A number of feminist writers over the past twenty years have attempted in quite thoughtful and sometimes provocative ways to salvage this term "hag," pointing out the sort of "outsiderhood" it connotes, along with the near mystical powers and insights usually attributed to women of a certain age. Behind the insult of "hag," as is the case with most stereotypical insults of this type, one perceives the fear and anxiety concerning the power of such women. If she is old and ugly, she has nothing to lose and so she is free to do whatever she wants. She is her own mistress, unfettered by expectation or tradition. She may pursue her own course, know her own self, act as she wishes whenever she wishes.

So, from a conventional perspective, it is extremely bad to be a "hag." But worse — oh, God, much worse — to be a "fag" hag. Not only are you a complete failure as a woman for not being sexually desirable to a heterosexual man, but, on top of it, you have chosen to consort primarily with "fags." It is beyond us here to go too deeply into the origins of this particular homophobic slur, but the origin of the word "faggot" is still shrouded in mystery and controversy. Some argue it sprang up during the late Middle Ages when sodomites were equated with heretics and burned at the stake with bundles of kindling called "faggots" lit at their feet. This association to burning survives even today in England, where a "fag" is both a cigarette as well as a homosexual and where, if you are "fagged," you are roughly equivalent to what we would called "burned out" or "wiped out." But of course, nowadays, particularly in the United States, "fag" survives nearly exclusively as a pejorative. With the expectable reaction common to most outsider groups when they embark upon a course of political and cultural self-determination, gay men have adopted and use the word "fag" among themselves as an ironic self-description.

Yet, the homophobic use of the term is clear: "fags" are not real men, and it is that implication which is embedded in the term "fag hag." A woman hangs around defective examples of masculinity because she herself is defective as a woman. She can't "get" a man so she turns to a "man substitute." "Fag hag" packs a powerful verbal punch — condemning the women for being less than "real" women, condemning the men she consorts with for being less than "real" men and condemning the friendship between the two as a pitiful substitute for a "real" relationship. We hasten to add that all this condemnation, of course, comes largely from people outside the friendship.

Telling It Like It Is

Now, the truly anxiety-provoking question for us is, why is *Fag Hags* the first thing most people suggest as a title for this book? Perhaps the shock value of the term, its inherent "oomph," keeps it alive and useful in speech. Certainly many of the gay men who refer to women as "hags" mean no disrespect in general, flipping the term around sometimes just for the sheer enjoyment of its assonance. These men are apt to enjoy being "bad boys," and there's nothing better than a term like this to get a bit of negative attention to revel in.

> *"If a woman has a lot of gay friends, I think she's smarter. I mean, who would you hang out with?"*

Laura reflects on her experience with the term. "I have never had anyone call me a fag hag, at least not to my face, but even prior to researching this book, I had heard the term repeatedly, and almost always from straight men. As I thought about it, however, I realized that these straight men who were using the phrase often had a similar attitude about other groups of men women chose to associate with. I think it has to do with competitiveness and with the need to explain why women would choose to spend time with other men. If a woman hangs out with a lot of good-looking gay men, then she is a "fag hag." If she hangs out with rich and successful men, she is a gold digger. If she hangs out with socially prominent men, she is a social climber. If she has a lot of famous friends, then she is a groupie. Maybe she only likes men of particular racial or ethnic varieties – I won't repeat their names for those women. And I don't think it is often intended seriously – it is more of an off-handed comment, not unlike the way women make off-handed comments when a straight male friend marries a much younger woman. Of course, taking the latter example, it is much less insulting to be called a "trophy wife" than a "fag hag." But my point is that I don't think straight men always see that difference – they aren't always sensitive to the extent to which the term is especially insulting to the woman and to the gay men who are her friends."

As we have noted, few of the women we interviewed referred to themselves as "fag hags," and gay men in general did not refer to their close female friends in this way, crediting themselves and their own relationships as something very much other than what that phrase conjures up. Yet whether a "fag hag" is an outdated relic from the disco era or a dysfunctional personality avoiding relationships with straight men, it is clear that if she exists, she represents the exception, a fractional minority, of the straight women who enjoy friendships with gay men. Though any relationship can be taken to an unhealthy extreme, most of the friendships between gay men and straight women are healthy, mutually fulfilling, and clearly entitled to more than the short shrift they usually receive.

Perhaps Patrick, who has a number of close female friends, summed it up best when he said, "I know some people talk about gay men and 'fag hags' in disparaging ways, but if a woman has a lot of gay friends, I think she's smarter. I mean, who would you hang out with? Gay men are more emotionally sustaining to straight women. They tend to be compassionate about what women go through, because we go through similar things. I think it shows good sense for a straight woman to have gay friends. 'Fag hag?' Call them what you will, they're my favorite people, and I don't think these women care what you call them. I think they'd laugh at the name; they're all so much more than that!"

11. Being There for Each Other

Having examined the challenges that straight women and gay men face in their friendships, we think it is far more fitting now to return to one of the most important things friends do for each other — help each other out. In line with

On a very basic level, the way that straight women and gay men come together in friendship to support each other through tough times seems quite natural.

our own earlier insight about gay men and women sharing in a certain kind of feminine perspective on the world, the fact is that we are very often "helpers." Women have most certainly been raised in our culture to nurture and give aid, and along with the arts, the helping professions are another place where women and gay men have come out in force — as nurses, as counselors, as teachers. Women and gay men are, in short, people who call upon their own capacity to give and to nourish.

Likewise, even the stereotypical association of women and gay men with gardening and cooking has to do with providing nourishment and growth. Rob talks about his own interests here. "A large part of my own professional life centers around helping others, or at least trying my best to, but many of my personal interests and hobbies have the same tenor to them. People know if they come to our house for dinner, they are going to be fed within an inch of their life, and I really have to say I enjoy growing what I serve, making the bread from scratch, really taking the time to serve something that has been made with a lot of care. So what I grow in my backyard and what I serve on the table comes from the same part of me that sits in my office and tries to help others find a way to be happier and more at peace."

Laura can attest to this aspect of Rob's nature, although she gently ribs him about it. "Yes, many a time have I enjoyed watching Rob cook a gourmet meal and tend to his garden while simultaneously talking a jumper off a high building with his cell phone in hand. But, in all seriousness, Rob truly does have a caring, nurturing quality I have seen in my most cherished gay friends. There is a selflessness about their affection that one associates, stereotypically, with mothers more than anyone else. And women love to fill this mother role, to pamper and fuss over those they love. This ability to provide care and comfort are important qualities women and gay men share."

So, on a very basic level, the way that straight women and gay men come together in friendship to support each other through tough times seems quite natural. It is almost a given, a part of a giving, loving nature that has brought them together in the first place.

Facing AIDS Together

In the past twenty years, of course, the times have been exceptionally tough for gay men. As we spoke to straight women about their friendships with gay men, the subject of AIDS and the needs of their many gay male friends in recent times were nearly always the first things they spoke of. Olivia's story of her friendship with Peter and his partner Quentin is typical of how a friendship like this functions in a time of crisis. "I met Peter through his partner Quentin who worked with me. We started to go out together socially, but when Quentin became sick with AIDS, I began to see much more of Peter and got to know him in a very different way. I really loved his sense of humor. I loved his

AIDS has taken a particular toll on the friendships between gay men and straight women, and it is not at all uncommon for the women who have endured this epidemic to have experienced the loss of nearly all their gay male friends.

sensibilities. We had a great time together. We had an interest in the arts — he comes from a very artistically talented family. So when Quentin got sick, I got together with Peter to do things for Quentin, and our relationship deepened."

Olivia paused, and then continued. "I saw the incredibly caring person Peter is. I grew in love and respect for him because of the way he took care of

Quentin. In the midst of this crisis, in all they went through together, the depth of Peter's personality emerged — his love, caring, his sense of humor, and all his emotions, both positive and negative. Peter cared for his partner in a way that I had never seen. I think the AIDS epidemic has brought this whole phenomenon to the fore — men taking caring of men in the way a woman usually takes care of someone. Peter's caring for Quentin moved and impressed me so deeply that when I thought of Peter, I had to say to myself, 'Now this is a real, total, full human being.' We shared so many things through Quentin's illness. The way Peter cared for Quentin was incredible to me, and it assured me that our future relationship would last through thick and thin. Peter is a dear and wonderful friend."

AIDS has taken a particular toll on the friendships between gay men and straight women, and it is not at all uncommon for the women who have endured this epidemic to have experienced the loss of nearly all their gay male friends. Heidi, an opera singer, told us, "When I think about all the bright spirits we have lost, all the wonderful, handsome, talented men I've worked and played with, I sometimes feel like I'm surrounded by this huge throng of loving ghosts. I knew them all for such a short period of time and now they are gone."

Like Heidi, women working in industries significantly represented by gay men, including entertainment, fashion, design, and the arts in general, have seen an entire generation of their best and most beloved colleagues disappear. Ask any of these women and they can tick off name after name of friends who have died.

And it is women who have been side by side with gay men from the beginning in the efforts to prevent, treat and give support to people with AIDS. Rob speaks of his work running an AIDS prevention program in San Francisco. "I was always aware of how many heterosexual women were involved in the work with me — the head of the AIDS Office; well-known entertainers; inspirational figures like Louise Hay; or Ruth Brinker, the woman who founded Project Open Hand to provide meals for the homebound. In fact, with the exception of the doctors and researchers, I can't really easily come up with the name of a straight man who was involved on the level of social support and prevention efforts. There must have been a few, of course, but nearly all the meetings I went to were always made up of gay men, lesbians and straight women. The same with the various informal support groups we formed to help individual people through the dying process: gay men, lesbians and straight women. And every year when we opened our program for internship applications, we would regularly get a lot of interest from various straight women who would always tell me in the interview with them that they really wanted to do something to make a difference, because they had lost so many friends themselves."

Yet there is one undeniably positive outgrowth of this harsh reality: since most gay men and many women have both lost so many dear friends to AIDS, the friends who remain are far less likely to take one another for granted. And those living with the disease provide a reality check that can enable their friends to see life in a new, strangely hopeful, light. Laura, whose close friend has lived with AIDS for several years, tell us this story. "My friend Charles has had AIDS since I met him five years ago. He has had good times and bad health-wise, has seen medical treatments work and then fail, has confronted crippling side-effects and devastating medical costs. He has been rejected by family members and by employers. And yet he is one of the most positive people I have ever met. His love for, and appreciation of, every moment of life puts all of my petty problems in perspective. I kept thinking about a man I was interested in who didn't seem to reciprocate, and Charles was incredulous: Why would I *waste time* on this man? Why would I *waste time* worrying about how my family might have mistreated me when I was young? He has an uncanny knack for focusing on what's important. The fact that he would choose me for a friend at this time in his life and would make it a priority to spend time with me, is incredibly meaningful for me. He has become my compass, the one who makes sure I am always headed in the right direction."

Pamela expressed similar sentiments. She told us, "I have a good friend with AIDS who asked me to travel across the country to spend Christmas with him. I really didn't want to go – I was busy at work and was too tired to travel. But all of a sudden it dawned on me – how many Christmases will we get to spend together? I hope it's fifty, but the reality is that it probably won't be. And so I went down there to spend Christmas with him. We took rolls of pictures, shared early morning breakfasts in our PJ's, and enjoyed long conversations that went on late into the night. And I thank God I will never have to regret having missed that time I spent with him."

Dealing With Other Life Crises Together

As is always the case with friends, much of what you give often comes back to you just when you need it. Olivia found that the friendship and support she was able to give Peter and Quentin came back to her during a difficult time in her own life. She recalled, "The following year I separated from my husband, and Peter was a wonderful, wonderful anchor for me. He was there for me, on the phone, in person, anything at all. He was someone I knew I could always call. He was clear, he was nonjudgmental. He was a wonderful source of support. We also deeply enjoy each other's sense of humor, which has sustained us both over the years."

A friend is someone who really takes the time to anticipate what a person needs most — a meal, a phone call, a hug, maybe even some time and distance.

And just as many women have helped and supported their friends and the wider gay community during the AIDS epidemic, so also have many gay men helped their female friends battle their own health crises, including not only AIDS, but most particularly breast and ovarian cancer. Laura notes that over the past few years, many of her gay friends have lost close female friends to cancer, including successful entertainers such as Nancy LaMott and Laurie Beechman who, like so many of their gay friends and fans, died far too young. Rob speaks of his friendship with Jill, whose best friend Judy died of breast cancer last year. "I tried very consciously in nearly every conversation to make sure I asked Jill how Judy was and how Jill herself was doing with Judy's slow decline. After all my own experiences with friends dying, I knew how hard it could be, and Jill doesn't always show her emotions. I really tried not to push but also to give her the chance to talk about it when she wanted. And when Judy died last year, I made sure to call Jill that whole week and check in. When someone is dying, you can't really do anything but be available. And breast cancer for women is a lot like HIV with gay men: you know you yourself are at risk for getting it, and on top of the grief you are feeling, there is always a lot of anxiety about your own health."

What comes through in all these stories, regardless of who is supporting whom or how, is the fact that facing a time of crisis together, being there for each other during tough times, strengthens the bond between friends. A friend is someone who, as these stories show, really takes the time to anticipate what a person needs most — a meal, a phone call, a hug, maybe even some time and distance. It is a truism but when times are tough, you do find out who your real friends are. For gay men and straight women, as we know, the real friends are often each other.

12. Understanding Each Other

 Ultimately what emerges from all these stories, reflections, experiences and notions about this special friendship, is the portrait of a relationship aptly summed up in the word "understanding." As gay men and straight women relate to each other, love each other, support each other, and spend their lives together, they establish a friendship that, in its way, provides a near-ideal model of a male-female relationship. As demonstrated by the many points of contact between gay men and straight women, and as eloquently expressed by many of the people we inter-

In the case of gay men and straight women, it seems that the things we understand about one another are so much more important than the things we don't.

viewed, it is striking and inspiring just how much understanding *is* possible between gay men and straight women. As Cynthia told us, "I think gay men and straight women can understand a lot more than straight men do. A lot of gay men live a much richer emotional life, just as a lot of women live a richer emotional life than straight men do in general. Which makes it a point of contact for gay men and women." Cynthia paused, then added, "The other thing is that many gay men look at the world a lot differently than straight men do, partially due to their being outside of the mainstream, subject to discrimination. There is a lot of commonality between gay men and women in that respect, and so there's a mutual understanding that straight white men just don't have a clue about. They have no idea what it is like to be discriminated against and even if it happened, they wouldn't recognize it anyway. I don't think they can understand what it is like to go to a meeting and say something and be ignored because you are not a white male. They just have no concept of it. Whereas, because of a general greater sensitivity, or because gay men are discriminated against in the same subtle, insidious ways women are, I think, gay men understand the dynamics of discrimination better."

Similarly, Patrick told us, "For women and gay men to understand each other is an easy step, because we have so much in common. Vis-à-vis the larger culture, we live in a very similar place. I think we are ostracized and excluded in much the same way; we are discounted and thought frivolous or weak. There are so many ways in which women are treated in the same way gay men are treated that we are instantly simpatico. I can't think of any straight women who I wouldn't be a little bit sympathetic to."

Yet many women we spoke with frankly acknowledged the limits of this understanding. When asked what she felt gay men could not understand about women, Olivia told us a story about an exchange she had with one of her friends. "One time at a party, my friend Casey was dressed 'in drag' in some feminine outfit, and someone there referred to him as 'she.' And he was kind of fooling around and referring to himself as a woman, and we got into this discussion about how he experienced himself as a woman. And I had to say to him, 'You know, I disagree with you identifying yourself as a woman. I don't think you can experience yourself that way, because in five minutes time, you can become a man again. You can play around with being a woman, but you aren't really a woman.' He listened to me, heard me, and responded, 'You are right. I can go back.'"

This issue of how much a man, even a gay man, can understand about what it's like to be a woman, also came up with Jacquie, who commented, "I never think that they get everything about being a woman, but what I really like is that they instinctively and from the gut get almost everything that is important."

Another experience that some women felt their gay male friends misunderstood was the actual physical experience of being a woman. When asked what she felt gay men didn't understand about women, Ellen said, "Certainly they don't understand the physiological limitations — the hormonal changes or the changes brought on by birth. I think there is a lot of emotional crossover, but the physical experience of being woman, I don't think most men can understand completely." Ingrid echoed this point about the limits of male understanding, when she pointed out, "Another thing gay men don't understand is the immediate drain of being a mother of young children. They don't see motherhood as part of their experience."

From gay men, we heard a similar give-and-take — the acknowledgment of how much can be mutually understood and yet how certain things remain mysterious and unseen, simply because the partners in these friendships are of different genders. Alan told us, "I don't even pretend to understand what women go through and what women deal with day to day as women. Being a gay man doesn't mean that I understand what women go through, because the average person isn't going to look at me and say, 'He's gay — let's treat him as a woman.' I think only 'like' people can really understand each other. But they can commiserate, very definitely."

And on the flipside, women can never fully understand what it means to be a gay man. As Laura puts it, "As a woman, I can never fully appreciate the pressures of having to be 'a real man' in today's society. And to be a homosexual in that society creates demands I will never have to encounter. So I am always amazed at how much understanding *is* possible between us and how infrequently misunderstandings occur. It's as if there is an unspoken agreement between us: we will understand what we can, and accept the rest."

Our conclusion? That the question: "can we understand each other?" has both a "yes" and a "no" answer. All of the men and women we spoke with felt certain things were clear points of contact while other aspects of what it means to be a woman or a man remains forever mysterious. Perhaps perfect understanding between any two people is an impossibility. But in the case of gay men and straight women, it seems that the things we understand about one another are *so* much more important than the things we don't.

The Gift of Acceptance

Yet friendships, our friendships, are about more than simple understanding. As Laura noted, we have to be willing to accept – and not judge — even the things we can't fully understand about one another. Patrick puts it this way: "One of the reasons straight women are attracted to gay men is that it's a safe haven; you know you're not going to be judged. What a lot of straight women get out of rela-

> *"We allow one another the space to be who we are, because we basically always know, underneath it all, where the other person is coming from."*

tionships with gay men is that they are finally in a friendship where they can explore themselves freely. This is possible because they are in a relationship with someone who doesn't judge them and who doesn't have an enormous number of preconceptions about what they should be." Pamela reinforced this point, when she said, "I have no interest in judging my gay friends and they have no interest in judging me. Absolute acceptance and unconditional love are part of the deal. I sometimes act in a way they find illogical or a bit obsessive, and they sometimes get a bit 'over the top' for my tastes. But we allow one another the space to be who we are, because we basically always know, underneath it all, where the other person is coming from."

Perhaps the reluctance to judge is understandable. Women all too frequently are judged on the basis of their external appearance, their marital status or number of children, and – very often – by their age. Gay men are judged by heterosexuals of both genders, by certain religious leaders and by the ignorant or intolerant of many descriptions. And most gay men and many women have had the experience of being "different," whether he was the only gay boy in school or she was the only female executive in the corporation. Most gay men and straight women we talked to had come to terms with themselves and the extent to which they were different from what others might expect. The last thing they would do is to impose such expectations on others. And so while similar natures, interests and inclinations form one pillar underlying the friendship, absolute acceptance forms the other. Together they support a relationship that can endure despite the judgments and expectations of others.

A Larger Vision

All the stories and reflections we have shared suggest, of course, one inescapable conclusion: there is much to celebrate in these unique and wonderful friendships. Differences, of course, exist between gay men and straight women besides the mere physical — our gender roles, our socialization, our individual quirks and quarrels, the occasional imbalance in sexual attraction. But what we consistently find is that all these

Men and women can indeed be friends in the truest and highest sense of that term.

differences are more than balanced out by the many similarities and points of contact — the delight in shared activities, the rich conversations and deep emotional sharing, the nearly unfailing attunement and ongoing emotional support, the endless sense of play, fun, and enjoyment, and the sheer exuberance of being able to be fully and completely oneself. Men and women can indeed be friends in the truest and highest sense of that term, and these real-life stories of how such friendships came to be and how they have been lived out over a lifetime stand as models of wholeness and partnership.

Every day, we all hear voices around us that urge us to seek satisfaction from a very narrow band of human relationships, that exalt marriage and romantic love above all else, and that tell us all our other relationships are less important or less fulfilling. But we hope this book makes clear just how wrong such a limited vision is. The deep knowledge, love, caring, affection and pleasure that comes from the special friendship between straight women and gay men is perhaps the best argument for taking time out from our search for the "perfect" mate and the "perfect" relationship. For if we do, and if we never take our friendships for granted, then men and women of any sexual orientation may find that the perfect relationship they seek isn't somewhere out there yet to be found but already exists. We may find that the people around us who love and care about us have already made us one half of that "perfect couple."

An ancient saying states that love comes from blindness, friendship from knowledge. Our own experiences and interviews have supported the truth of this observation. Gay men and straight women are friends, because, on some very fundamental level, they share a deep knowledge of each other, a connection that really can be described by no other term than "soul mate." Our hope is that the stories and reflections shared here have affirmed your own friendships and led you to a renewed appreciation of those with whom you share your life. Both as authors and as friends, we hope we have accomplished our goal of helping you celebrate and live out more fully the marvelous, baffling, amazing complexity of the real nature of love in all its manifestations.

Notes

[1] Deborah Tannen, *You Just Don't Understand: Women and Men in Conversation* (New York: Ballantine, 1991).

[2] John Gray, *Men Are from Mars, Women Are from Venus,* (New York: HarperCollins, 1992).

[3] John Preston, *Hometowns: Gay Men Write About Where They Belong* (New York: Dutton, 1991), xiii.

[4] Dan Anderson and Maggie Berman, *Sex Tips for Straight Women from a Gay Man* (New York: HarperCollins, 1997), xv-xvi.

[5] E. F. Benson, *Make Way for Lucia* (New York: Harper & Row, 1977), x.

[6] Rebecca Nahas and Myra Turley, *The New Couple: Women and Gay Men* (New York: Seaview Books, 1979).

[7] Robert Rodi, *Fag Hag* (New York: Plume, 1993), p. 1.

About the Authors

Robert H. Hopcke is a Licensed Marriage and Family Therapist in private practice in Berkeley, California, and is currently the Director of the Center for Symbolic Studies, a non-profit organization he founded with others to further the study of psychology, sociology, and religion. Along with his numerous articles and reviews published throughout the world, he is the author of *There Are No Accidents: Synchronicity and the Stories of Our Lives; A Guided Tour of the Collected Works of C.G. Jung; Jung, Jungians and Homosexuality,* and two other books.

Laura Rafaty is a writer, theatrical producer, corporate executive and attorney. She produced a number of plays including *Twilight Los Angeles* (On and Off-Broadway, Tony Award nomination, Obie Award), *Sylvia* (San Francisco and Canada), *Jeffrey* (Los Angeles), and *Gate of Heaven* (national tour), and is on the Board of Directors of the Drama Dept, an off-Broadway theatre group. She works as an attorney and corporate executive in California and maintains her theatrical production office in New York City.

E-mail Rob and Luara at robandlaura@hotmail-com.

About the Press

Wildcat Canyon Press publishes books that embrace such subjects as friendship, spirituality, women's issues, and home and family, all with a focus on self-help and personal growth. Great care is taken to create books that inspire reflection and improve the quality of our lives. Our books invite sharing and are frequently given as gifts.

For a catalog of our publications, please write:

Wildcat Canyon Press
2716 Ninth Street
Berkeley, California 94710
Phone (510) 848-3600
Fax (510) 848-1326
Visit us at: www.wildcatcanyon.com
E-mail: info@wildcatcanyon.com

More Wildcat Canyon Titles

MOVING FROM FEAR TO COURAGE: TRANSCENDENT MOMENTS
OF CHANGE IN THE LIVES OF WOMEN
A fascinating and inspiring look at brief moments of
insight, which allow women to live beyond their fears and
change their lives forever.
Cheryl Fischer and Heather Waite
$13.95 ISBN 1-885171-50-1

IN THE DRESSING ROOM WITH BRENDA: A FUN AND PRACTI-
CAL GUIDE TO BUYING SMART AND LOOKING GREAT
Personal Shopping advice from Brenda Kinsel, the
author of *40 over 40*, and every woman's favorite image
consultant.
Brenda Kinsel
$16.95 ISBN 1-885171-51-X

40 OVER 40: 40 THINGS EVERY WOMAN OVER 40 NEEDS TO
KNOW ABOUT GETTING DRESSED
An image consultant shows women over forty how to love
what they wear and wear what they love.
Brenda Kinsel
$16.95 ISBN 1-885171-42-0

girlfriends GET TOGETHER: FOOD, FROLIC AND FUN TIMES!
The ultimate party planner from the best-selling authors of
the girlfriends series
Carmen Renee Berry, Tamara Traeder, and Janet Hazen
$19.95 ISBN 1-885171-53-6